The Roots of Low Achievement

The Roots of Low Achievement

Where to Begin Altering Them

Sandra Stotsky

ROWMAN & LITTLEFIELD
Lanham • Boulder • New York • London

Published by Rowman & Littlefield
An imprint of The Rowman & Littlefield Publishing Group, Inc.
4501 Forbes Boulevard, Suite 200, Lanham, Maryland 20706
www.rowman.com

6 Tinworth Street, London SE11 5AL

British Library Cataloguing in Publication Information Available

Library of Congress Cataloging-in-Publication Data

Names: Stotsky, Sandra, author.
Title: The roots of low achievement : where to begin altering them / Sandra
    Stotsky.
Description: Lanham : Rowman & Littlefield, [2019] | Includes bibliographical
    references.
Identifiers: LCCN 2019004904 (print) | LCCN 2019011100 (ebook) | ISBN
    9781475849899 (Electronic) | ISBN 9781475849875 (cloth : alk. paper) |
    ISBN 9781475849882 (pbk. : alk. paper)
Subjects: LCSH: Academic achievement—Government policy—United States. |
    Public schools—United States. | Education and state—United States.
Classification: LCC LB1062.6 (ebook) | LCC LB1062.6 .S775 2019 (print) | DDC
    371.2/07—dc23
LC record available at https://lccn.loc.gov/2019004904

♾ ™ The paper used in this publication meets the minimum requirements of American National Standard for Information Sciences Permanence of Paper for Printed Library Materials, ANSI/NISO Z39.48-1992.

Printed in the United States of America

To those in this country who want their public schools to prepare their children and grandchildren for the voluntary activities of self-government.

Contents

Preface

Once, parents were responsible for preparing their children for kindergarten or first grade. Teachers were responsible for teaching children to read, write, and calculate. But not all parents lived up to their end of the deal, so policy makers added parents' responsibilities to the growing list of things teachers and school programs were responsible for, in addition to the three Rs.

With the shift in responsibilities has come a shift in blame. When kids from low-income families haven't learned how to read by grade 3, policy makers tend to blame poverty, not the teaching methods for early reading. But if primary-grade teachers are using methods like "Whole Language," "Balanced Literacy," or "Guessing from Context" to teach beginning reading and many students are failing to learn how to read fluently (or how to read at all) by grade 3, then the culprit *is*, at least in part, what teachers were taught to do in professional development or teacher-preparation programs.

At the same time, some education researchers have been looking outside the education box altogether. In a study published in 1996, Laurence Steinberg said, "We think the school-reform movement has been focusing on the wrong things. The problem isn't the schools; it's the disengagement of parents and a peer culture that demeans high academic performance."[1] If you believe that education reform has failed to turn low achievers into high achievers in the past fifty years because reformers have focused on the wrong things (e.g., holding administrators and teachers accountable for students' scores on state tests that these teachers and administrators didn't create, review, or approve), then there are grounds for hope. The roots of low achievement can be altered if education policy makers refocus. But on what?

Steinberg wasn't talking about only the students we call low achievers or children of low-income parents—students whom the Elementary and Secondary Education Act sought to help in 1965. Steinberg was talking about most

American students. He was pointing to a problem that education policy makers can't admit to. Most American students, including those who are called "privileged" or "high achievers," are not doing as well academically as they should be compared to their peers in other developed countries.

Many Americans believe that education policy makers have spent fifty years focusing on the wrong targets: low achievers. Not only have these policy makers *not* turned low achievers into high achievers, but they have also failed to strengthen academically both the K–12 curriculum and teachers and administrators in our schools. In fact, they have weakened the school curriculum for all students while pretending they were giving low achievers access to a "high-quality curriculum." And they have also managed to convince a lot of people that the real problem with low achievers is their teachers. They are bigots, we are told, mainly because most are "white." If you believe that, then you need to read this book. The roots of low achievement do not lie primarily in teachers' attitudes.

NOTE

1. Quoted in Mary B. W. Tabor, "Comprehensive Study Finds Parents and Peers Are Most Crucial Influences on Students," *New York Times*, August 7, 1996, https://www.nytimes.com/1996/08/07/us/comprehensive-study-finds-parents-peers-are-most-crucial-influences-students.html.

Introduction

THE FIRST FIVE CHAPTERS

Chapter 1 highlights the major changes in American high schools during the twentieth century that shaped their academic functions. High schools were once the pride and joy of most American communities. But as an educational institution, they may not be salvageable today because of changes to teacher qualifications, secondary course content, and the amount of time most students are willing to spend reading and writing outside of school. Most changes during the twentieth century reduced the content of academic coursework and time spent on this coursework by teachers and students.

The 1965 Moynihan report and the 1966 Coleman report conclude that students' academic achievement is more a reflection of their family background than their teachers' and schools' efforts. Almost all policies and programs created since then to address low achievers and the children of low-income families (interchangeable students, it seems, in education policy makers' minds) have focused on educational initiatives and ignored the findings of both reports. And these policies and programs have all turned up short, despite the time and money spent implementing them, as well as the reams of paperwork expected of local school administrators.

Like a person who looks for a car key under a streetlight even though he knows he lost the key elsewhere (because there is light there, he explains), stubborn policy makers at the US Department of Education, Congress, and civil rights organizations have insisted on holding K–12 teachers and administrators accountable for the achievement of low-performing students. But they have all known that our educational institutions could do little to address a problem the schools didn't create.

Chapter 2 looks briefly at several policies, programs, and research topics that educators have spent their energy on in the past half-century, none of which was directly related to the findings of the 1966 Coleman report:

1. benefits of increases in per-pupil spending
2. teaching effectiveness
3. pedagogy for skills, strategies, and processes
4. ways to distort or omit content
5. size of schools attended by low achievers
6. turnaround models to transform low-achieving schools
7. various K–12 curricular and staffing policies and programs

Chapter 3 discusses the characteristics of the teachers of minority children, as described in the Coleman report, and what the report means by "teacher quality." Chapter 3 uses a current flap over a state-based teacher licensure test in elementary mathematics to raise an unanswered question: Why did Congress not try to strengthen all teacher-preparation programs, either as part of the first authorization of the Elementary and Secondary Education Act in 1965 or right after the release of the Coleman report in 1966?

Chapter 4 highlights nonschool factors that may be related to low achievement, as noted in either the Moynihan report or the Coleman report.

Chapter 5 looks at some topics related to school achievement that noneducation scientists, medical and public health researchers, legal scholars, sociologists, anthropologists, and psychologists have explored since 1966. In experimental research and scholarly papers, noneducation researchers have examined (1) technologies used in and out of school, (2) adolescent sleep needs, (3) school discipline, (4) poverty, (5) family culture, and (6) academic motivation. Their work suggests that there may be many possible influences on student achievement.

THE LAST FIVE CHAPTERS

Chapter 6 notes that philanthropists have already spent a lot of money trying to address low-achieving schools, and they plan to spend even more. But judging from scores on the National Assessment of Educational Progress (NAEP) tests, there has been little improvement in the academic status of low-achieving students in this country as a result of private philanthropy in the past four decades.

A detailed study of how much money American philanthropists have given to low achievers in recent decades reveals many criticisms, including the following: (1) Outside money evades public scrutiny and discussion, leaving parents in the dark about the specific policies these strings have imposed on schools. (2) Philanthropists typically have no accountability to local parents or the public at large, even though their actions affect almost all students. And (3) their private gifts are often intended as leverage for matching public funds but with little if any voter discussion or approval of the donors' specific intentions.

Chapter 7 notes that education policy makers don't learn much from both failed *and* effective policies. If policy makers claim that their policies have failed because of, for example, "insufficient funding," then they may not learn much from these failures. Additionally, if policy makers don't like either the effective policies or the policy makers responsible for them, then they also may not learn anything from their successes. (To this day national researchers can't acknowledge the success or effectiveness of the philosophy in Massachusetts—that an emphasis on reading good literature improves all kids' reading skills. It's hard to find any official in the National Council of Teachers of English or in English education saying this.)

Chapter 8 points out how the public has been misled through cover-ups about "successful" policies that most likely would have been viewed otherwise as failures. For example, Common Core's damaging standards are almost always referred to by the media as "rigorous." It is not clear to what extent the public has been deliberately deceived, and it is not easy to find successes portrayed as failures; however, failures are often portrayed as successes or as muddled in outcomes. When something works, it is hard not to see it.

Chapter 8 looks at deception involving inflated grades, marks, or credit for the coursework; course titles that suggest more was to be taught than what actually was; biased sources of information; missing research; distorted research findings; relevant information withheld from parents; a new, non-evidence-based high school diploma; and the exclusion of academic experts in determining college readiness.

Chapter 9 raises questions about closing "gaps" as an educational goal. It suggests what policy makers and educators (desperate teachers, in many cases) may do to try to close gaps when their evaluations, reputations, or jobs depend on it. They may teach less content to higher achievers in order to equalize achievement between higher and low achievers or ignore what college teaching faculty say college readiness means. Chapter 9 then suggests why the K–12 school curriculum changed after 1970 and paved the way for an obsession with gap closing.

The final chapter of this book addresses two factors that are not in the 1965 Moynihan report, the 1966 Coleman report, and in most subsequent education research. This chapter first highlights the research reported in *Beyond the Classroom: Why School Reform Has Failed and What Parents Need to Do*, published in 1996. This book implicitly proposes *student effort* as a central factor in academic achievement, and its title makes it clear that the authors don't find much to say in favor of the "education reforms" of the past half-century.

Unlike many research reports today, *Beyond the Classroom* comments on the academic success of Asian students, noting that they "perform better in school because they work harder, try harder, and are more interested in achievement—the very same factors that contribute to school success among *all* ethnic groups." The question that readers must answer for themselves is why policy makers at the US Department of Education, the members of Congress who voted for the 2015 reauthorization of the 1965 Elementary and Secondary Education Act, and the many philanthropists in this country with a professed interest in education attribute low achievement of black and Hispanic students to discrimination by teachers, school administrators, and local boards of education.

The other factor unexamined in research or reports issued in the past half-century is a student's civic identity. Most educators know that the US history curriculum has collapsed, if not altogether disappeared, in K–12 schools. The Constitution and other founding documents are no longer required reading in new social studies standards, issued by the National Council for the Social Studies. Yet, US history has always been a major part of a curriculum for civic education in this country. A civics curriculum teaches all students, including low achievers, about informed citizenship and promotes the idea that all citizens are politically equal to each other, regardless of academic achievement. This ideal has been abandoned, though, and it desperately needs to be restored as the goal of K–12 public education if we are to begin to alter the roots of low achievement.

Chapter One

The Deteriorating Curriculum in American High Schools

The academic quality of public education in this country had been declining since well before World War II, according to such critics as historian Arthur Bestor; Admiral Hyman Rickover, a developer of the nuclear-powered submarine; and educator Rudolph Flesch, who wrote the 1955 best-selling book *Why Johnny Can't Read*.[1] Two books, one in 1957 and the other in 1967, by James B. Conant, a president of Harvard University and former chemistry professor, urged the consolidation of small public high schools and advocated for stronger mathematics and science curricula in all public high schools.[2] There was also a brief spurt of congressional attention to curriculum reform after the launching of *Sputnik* in 1957, culminating in the National Defense Education Act (NDEA) in 1958. NDEA institutes took place all over the country, as scholars, scientists, and teachers together tried to change textbooks and pedagogy in K–12 science, mathematics, foreign languages, and English curricula in particular:

> [NDEA] was designed to fulfill two purposes. First, it was designed to provide the country with specific defense-oriented personnel. This included providing federal help to foreign language scholars, area studies centers, and engineering students. Second it provided financial assistance—primarily through the National Defense Student Loan program—for thousands of students who would be part of the growing numbers enrolling at colleges and universities in the 1960s.[3]

The curriculum reform "movement" (a way to designate *Sputnik*-era programs and NDEA institutes) faded so rapidly that only those who were involved in the institutes are apt to remember that this country once sought to strengthen the school curriculum. After the release of the Moynihan report in March 1965, passage of the Elementary and Secondary Education Act (ESEA) in April 1965, and the release of the Coleman report in 1966, attention and money moved to the education of the children of low-income families. (In the eyes of education policy makers, low-income families always had low-achieving students. They still don't know what to make of the academic success of the children of poor Asian immigrants and refugees.)

After World War II, the school curriculum continued to weaken for many students (especially in English and history) but so gradually and with so many justifications that few noticed or cared, even when scores on the SAT verbal and math tests sank dramatically in 1963. Some claimed that the broadening pool of test-takers was the culprit, even though the number of highly proficient students also declined; others claimed that the simplification of school textbooks was the reason for the decline. (Was it done to address the increasing enrollment of weaker students in our high schools and colleges after 1950?)

There were few recommendations to strengthen K–12 public education *after* 1963. That idea was included as a purpose of ESEA in 1965 but was forgotten in subsequent reauthorizations of ESEA. *Equity* and *access* became the buzzwords used by sympathetic educators and others to describe their goals, mainly for minority students. It is puzzling why civil rights groups wanted minority kids to have greater access to an increasingly weaker K–12 curriculum. This chapter highlights major changes in the structure and curriculum of our high schools in the first half of the twentieth century and their academic decline in the past half-century.

AMERICAN HIGH SCHOOLS BEFORE WORLD WAR II

Laws on compulsory education and child labor began in the nineteenth century, but the curriculum in "comprehensive American high schools" drastically evolved during the twentieth century. Junior high schools first emerged at the turn of the twentieth century, followed by the development of four curriculum sequences ("tracks") in grade 9 in these new junior high schools or in regular high schools. Teacher licensure tests were required at first for K–8 but eventually extended through grade 12.

Enormous Growth in High Schools and Enrollment

The curriculum had been largely unchanged since the Puritans established Boston Latin School in 1635 and Harvard College in 1636. Because of the growth in high school enrollment around the turn of the twentieth century, the first major changes to the school curriculum began then. For example, at the beginning of the twentieth century, Latin and Greek were replaced with science in many schools.

Until around 1900, few students attended high school, fewer graduated, and even fewer went on to college. National child labor laws were passed at that time to prevent most young adolescents from working in factories, and compulsory school attendance laws (beginning in mid-nineteenth-century Massachusetts) kept students in school past the elementary grades until usually fourteen or sixteen years of age.

Public high schools, mostly financed by local communities, grew like Topsy after 1900. In many cities, these schools largely enrolled the children of new immigrants. With increasing numbers of students attending these high schools instead of dropping out (with parental permission) at age fourteen to work on a family farm or in a family business, the reform policies to prolong attendance in public schools were considered successful.

Development of Junior High Schools

It's hard to believe today that the junior high school was an innovation after the turn of the twentieth century. It was developed to provide a transition from the ubiquitous nineteenth-century K–8 grammar school to a 9–12 high school. By severing grades 7 and 8 from K–8 grammar schools and combining them with grade 9 classes in the high school, educators hoped to establish a distinct school that was discipline-oriented enough to prepare students for subject-centered high school coursework—coursework that would, in turn, prepare future engineers, ministers, and lawyers for college-level work.

The teachers in a junior high school were expected to be as trained in their subjects as high school teachers were, although it eventually became hard to find a math teacher capable of teaching Algebra I in grade 8 or 9, unless a mathematically qualified teacher was willing to stay and teach math in a school filled with young students. As a reform to increase retention, junior high schools were a success story. However, many students did not go on to high school, and there was no grade 8 graduation.

Development of Four Curriculum Sequences

To appeal to students before grade 9 (i.e., before they could drop out of school), junior high schools developed several curriculum sequences starting in grade 9 for students to choose from. As a history of the development of the junior high schools puts it,

> In addition to giving college-bound youths earlier access to college preparatory work, educators in these schools sought to entice greater numbers of non-college-bound youths to stay in school at least through grade nine by offering them commercial, domestic, and vocational curricula. By 1920 the number of

junior high schools in the United States had grown to 883. By the 1940s more
than half of the nation's young adolescents attended a junior high school, and
by 1960 four out of five did so.[4]

Clearly, the idea was to get grade 8 students to choose one of four curriculum tracks so that students might be interested enough to complete grade 9,
enroll in high school, take the high school coursework provided in one of
those "tracks," and graduate. The educators' goal was to try to keep "non-
college-bound" students in school for as many years as possible by attracting
them with a choice of high school program, however limited these four major
curriculum choices might seem in the twenty-first century.

The curriculum sequences were in most high schools by 1920 and lasted
for about fifty years. Regardless of whether students or their parents had a
choice of track (it is not clear), these sequences can be viewed as part of a
successful school retention reform (as well as successful job preparation in
the commercial track for the many women who became bookkeepers, secre-
taries, and accountants).

Development of the Comprehensive American High School

Before World War I, only about 3 percent of Americans went to high school,
according to census figures on the school-age population—and more girls
than boys attended high school until the 1960s, when enrollment rates equal-
ized. Before the war, most Americans lived in small towns or counties that
either had their own small high school (often with fewer than one hundred
graduates each year) or paid tuition for their able students to attend a private
academy, as many New England towns did.

The "comprehensive" high school—one school for all those whose parents wanted taxpayer-supported public education—was as uniquely an
American institution, as was the public library, the community college, and
the local volunteer fire station. All high school curriculum sequences un-
folded under one large roof because that was what the public seemed to want.

A few very large cities (e.g., Boston, Philadelphia, Providence, New
York) had "examination" high schools for very able students, and most also
had "vocational" schools for children who couldn't handle an academic curriculum. Comprehensive high schools have been widely judged as a successful reform in a society without a titled aristocracy. Most adolescents attended
or graduated from one and left school as English-language speakers, readers,
and writers.

Teacher Licensure Tests as Tests of Pedagogical Judgment

The growth of tests for teacher licensure (certification) in the 1920s corre-
lates to the growth in public high schools across the country. Urban teaching

positions were far more desirable than rural teaching positions, so cities often gave their own tests in order to find the most qualified candidates. Soon the dilemma at the heart of teacher licensure morphed into an argument about their purpose. Were they intended to predict teaching effectiveness or to assess teachers' command of the subjects they would teach? Were they supposed to protect those enrolled in education schools that awarded the certificates, or did they protect K–12 students from academically incompetent teachers?

Education schools generally won that battle, and licensure tests became heavily oriented to pedagogy for K–8 teachers, despite disagreement by testing companies on their purpose and how validity was established.[5] Most twentieth-century teacher-licensing tests and policies *cannot* be judged as effective if their purpose was to protect children from academically incompetent teachers. High schools that could hire unlicensed teachers (as in Massachusetts until after World War II) tended to hire strong graduates of liberal arts colleges.

AMERICAN HIGH SCHOOLS AFTER WORLD WAR II

The rigor of the general curriculum in American high schools continued its downward spiral a decade or so after World War II and through the twenty-first century. Although the college track at first strengthened mathematics and science coursework and advanced placement (AP) courses were developed for able students, the academic level of the general curriculum was lowered, chiefly in the reading level of the literary and nonliterary English texts and the textbooks used in other subjects. Middle schools (for grades 5–8) replaced many junior high schools (for grades 7–9).

The SAT verbal and math scores plummeted in 1963. The Carnegie Corporation funded a committee to develop what became the National Assessment of Educational Progress (NAEP), or the Nation's Report Cards. Release of *A Nation at Risk* in 1983 alarmed the country about the quality of public education and showed that some people were still keeping an eye on the K–12 curriculum. In 1988, Congress established and funded the National Assessment Governing Board (NAGB), allowing the Department of Education to appoint the people who would set NAEP testing policies.

A standards movement began with the release of national mathematics curriculum standards in 1989. Their purpose was both to unify the math curriculum across the country and to guide mathematics pedagogy. Eventually, the drive for national content standards changed to a push for state-developed sets of content standards (known as "standards-based reform").

By 2010, the movement for content standards evolved into national skills-oriented standards and tests based on them, part of a centralizing movement for educational policy in the 2000s. Closing academic gaps between politically defined demographic groups became the chief mission of public education and the goal that schools would have to seek if they wanted federal money, which left many parents unhappy with their own public schools.

Development of Middle Schools

After World War II, middle schools were developed to address the problems that critics saw in junior high schools: Junior high schools weren't different enough from high schools to satisfy child development experts, and rapid changes in early adolescence made for a heavy concentration in one building of youngsters with high energy levels and growing romantic interests. To create a middle school, grade 9 was put back into the high school (unless a separate school for grades 8 and 9 was created), and grades 7 and 8 were combined with 5 and 6, leaving a 4/4/4 structure for K–12 education (and sometimes for teacher licensure).

Most students also leave middle school and go on to high school, so grade 8 is often the de facto culmination of an elementary course of studies (4/4) instead of part of a secondary sequence in each subject leading to grade 9. Mathematics study, in particular, can be strongly affected. For example, Algebra I in a junior high school belongs in either grade 8 or 9; it doesn't belong in a middle school ending in grade 8 if the grade 8 curriculum is seen as the end of an elementary sequence, not the first step toward advanced mathematics coursework. The middle school's lack of emphasis on academic goals became clearer after teachers' licenses for grades 5–8 reflected pedagogy as much as or more than content.

Eventually, many middle schools came to be taught by a teacher with a middle school license, and this became the most serious problem with middle school: the limited academic qualifications of the teaching staff. After the formation of a middle school, academically trained secondary teachers headed for the high school as soon as a position was available; they were not licensed to teach grades 5 and 6 and did not want to be. In a K–8 grammar school, a teacher *could* have a college major or minor in a discipline, and a grade 8 English teacher would expect adult-level reading skills. But a teacher also could have a major or minor in education.

In contrast, many middle school teachers were often little more than glorified elementary teachers—elementary-trained teachers licensed for K–6 who had added a license for teaching grades 7 and 8. Depending on the state, adding a middle school license often meant no more than taking a course in adolescent development or a survey course in a subject taught in a middle school or both.

Sometimes, in rural areas, a teacher licensed to teach K–8 was still available and was now even more desirable to school administrators because she could teach legally any school subject in K–8 at any grade (theoretically only in a self-contained classroom). It didn't matter to state or federal officials or to school administrators that the middle-school-licensed teacher in grade 7 or 8 didn't know much of the content taught in those grades until her academic deficiencies showed up in a standards-based environment.

For example, long before 2000, Boston would not hire any teacher with a middle school license for grades 7 and 8. In Arkansas, a large rural state, the state's department of education around 2009 developed an "endorsement" in Algebra I to enable its already-licensed teachers in grade 8 to become qualified to teach Algebra I in grade 8 if willing to undertake more academic training. The state wanted more able students for the advanced mathematics and science courses in its high schools. AP courses were already mandated for its high schools, regardless of whether there were students qualified for them.

Development of the Nation's Report Cards

Most Americans had no more than a grade 8 education before World War I, but large numbers had a high school diploma by World War II. However, the technology developed in World War II required its users to have much more than a traditional high school education in mathematics and science. After World War II, the time seemed right for strengthening the secondary school. And as if to emphasize a need for curriculum reform and recruitment of stronger teachers for grades K–12, the SAT verbal and math test scores sharply declined in 1963.

Some education researchers believed that the cause of this decline was not the broadening of the test-taking population because the number of students with a high level of proficiency also declined. Others weren't sure what the causes of the decline were, although they suspected that the lowered reading levels of school textbooks (mostly in response to teachers' requests) was the culprit. The most able high school students were reading textbooks with lowered reading levels, and it wouldn't have mattered what researchers said.

Schools wanted more money for "reform." The need to address impoverished African American communities and schools on tribal reservations meant that the focus of educational initiatives could not be stronger curricula in science and mathematics, and few wanted to know why textbook reading levels had been lowered.

NDEA efforts fizzled very quickly—too quickly—as if this country didn't have the resources to both strengthen the K–12 curriculum for all students *and* address low achievers. The "war on poverty" in schools that began in 1965 with the first authorization of the Elementary and Secondary Education Act never ended, mainly because it was ultimately not really about poverty.[6] By the beginning of the twenty-first century, it was clearly about the centralization of public policy at the Department of Education. A 2015 essay in *Education Next* by Arne Duncan's chief of staff, Joanne Weiss, makes that clear.[7]

After the decline in SAT scores in 1963, the Carnegie Corporation of New York was concerned about the strength of the school curriculum and gave successive grants to a special committee in 1964 for the development of what became known as National Assessment of Educational Progress (NAEP) tests, or *The Nation's Report Cards.*[8] Testing of random but stratified samples of students began in 1969 on a voluntary basis.

It wasn't until 1988 and the establishment of the National Assessment Governing Board (NAGB) that Congress put its stamp on the whole effort. However, Congress showed little interest in the caliber of the nation's teachers until the 1998 reauthorization of the Higher Education Act (HEA), which required states to report teacher licensure test results annually, and the 2001 reauthorization of ESEA (known as No Child Left Behind, or NCLB), which compelled school districts to pay attention to teachers' academic backgrounds (to determine if they were highly qualified teachers). After 2001, all states had to participate in NAEP testing.

Skills as Standards

The influence of a report titled *A Nation at Risk* in 1983 on this country's understanding of the quality of its public schools cannot be overstated. It became the basis for the development of standards to improve public education. These standards differ from the model syllabi (with specific topics) that many countries provide to guide construction of secondary courses.

In 1989, the National Council of Teachers of Mathematics released its first set of curriculum standards—the first professional educational organization to do so. Congress then decided to go with content standards developed by national professional organizations. Unfortunately, they tended to reflect chiefly the influence of educators, not scholars or academic experts. After a national battle over biased history standards, national academic standards developed by professional education and discipline-based organizations were abandoned in favor of state-developed standards. However, these, too, were developed mainly by educators chosen by state departments of education, not by scholars or academic experts.

Worse yet, most state standards turned out to be useless in turning low achievers into higher achievers or in equalizing educational opportunities within a state. According to national and international tests, only one state (Massachusetts) developed standards that contributed to a stronger school curriculum and to academic gains in all demographic groups of students. But exactly what this state did was ignored by philanthropists and education policy makers and was not studied by education researchers.

Because of NCLB regulations, low achievers were consistently identified as members of specific racial and ethnic groups (they were not considered just low achievers), especially on NAEP tests. National policy makers for political reasons decided that gap closing was the goal of public education and promoted test-based accountability. Eventually, content standards were mostly discarded in favor of skills or "competencies," as in the Common Core project, to enable all students to graduate from grade 12 "college-ready." However, it was and still is not clear what "college readiness" or scores based on Common Core–aligned tests mean.

Decline in the Academic Quality of Teachers

Because of growing career alternatives in the 1950s and 1960s, teacher shortages developed. Liberal arts graduates with advanced degrees increasingly sought other careers instead of teaching in public schools. (In contrast, many high schools in the 1930s hired unemployed PhDs.) State legislatures required increases in pedagogy credits (not academic credits).

K–12 teachers began to request easier-to-read materials, and publishers responded by lowering reading levels of textbooks. Less difficult texts replaced high-school-level literary and nonliterary readings, often in the name of multiculturalism, to accommodate the larger number of academically weaker students who now populated high schools because of the curriculum sequences put into grade 9 years earlier to interest non-college-bound students. By the late 1960s, if there was any interest in a stronger curriculum, no one knew how to implement one for any group of students. Yet, "experts" on educational issues sprang up like mushrooms after a rain.

Growth of Nonexpert "Experts" in Education

Before the strong focus on low achievement in the 1970s, experts were generally people with recognized achievement or experience in K–12 schools (as administrators or as teachers) or academic subject matter specialists. Academic experts and academically strong teachers had typically been the participants in NDEA institutes. After the collapse of NDEA efforts to strengthen the entire school curriculum and the turn of attention to low achievers, "experts" in education multiplied like rabbits but rarely had expertise in anything educational. They may have achieved recognition for an idea, for publishing research, for holding faculty positions in education schools, or any combination of these, but they rarely had established records of increasing academic achievement in any group of students or in strengthening the school curriculum.

In the early 1950s, James B. Conant, longtime president of Harvard University and clearly interested in strengthening high school teachers and curriculum, visited hundreds of high schools with a team of colleagues to figure out how to strengthen them. Supported by the Carnegie Corporation, he recommended an optimal size of about 750 students in high schools and regional consolidation of small public high schools so they could hire stronger teachers and put stronger science and mathematics coursework in place.

In contrast, in the early 2000s, leading philanthropists Bill and Melinda Gates urged breaking up large urban high schools into smaller schools of about two hundred students, and as far as we know, they have never visited any of the schools before or after. Neither had any experience in public schools. Moreover, Gates's small-schools initiative was abandoned once good test scores were not consistently forthcoming.

Founder of Amazon Jeff Bezos announced in late 2018 that he would spend two billion dollars on "Montessori-inspired" preschools.[9] It's too soon for information on what this businessman knows about Montessori teachers and preschools or how academically strong his preschools will be.

Reduction in Academic Demands

Almost every new strategy introduced to teachers in the 1960s and afterward has resulted in less content taught to *all* students. Most traditional practices were also found wanting. Educators were ingenious in finding ways to reduce the content of the school curriculum, but they were spectacularly unsuccessful in showing prospective teachers how to teach low achievers to read, write, and calculate—in effect, to become higher achievers. The following strategies have been implemented with mixed results:

- *Block scheduling* is controversial today because it is not clear that longer time blocks mean higher academic performance for all students; instead, it often reduces the time available for teaching a subject.[10] Students need a lot of practice *writing*, but when it is mostly done in school, it takes up a lot of instructional time that was once used in other ways.
- *Mastery learning* allows for "detracking," but it also may leave faster learners twiddling their thumbs until slower learners catch up. Detracked classrooms mean a mix of weaker and stronger students. The research doesn't support the practice for effective math teaching.
- *Group projects* (i.e., project-based learning, or PBL) may consume much of the time that was once used for direct instruction. They may also take advantage of the most capable students in a group, who end up doing the teacher's work, essentially as unpaid assistants. Teachers say it is difficult to teach foreign languages and mathematics in schools promoting PBL. Some subjects need sequenced instruction and regular practice, but the

widespread presumption of enhanced academic motivation from PBL may override subject matter learning requirements. [11]

- *Homework* in the form of reading and writing outside of class time has been drastically reduced for most students for many reasons: Students have to work; students have to take care of siblings after school; students need time after school for athletic and other extracurricular activities; students can't concentrate in noisy homes or neighborhoods; students have chores; homework is often busywork; homework may not be corrected by the teacher; and students spend a lot of time on long bus rides to and from school. However, as most high school teachers indicate, homework in English is still necessary for the supplementary reading and writing that college readiness requires.

- *Practice* in spelling or arithmetic may be considered a waste of student time by some educators but usually not by elementary teachers. Few music teachers or athletic coaches think practice is a waste of time for learning a musical instrument or a sport.

By the end of the twentieth century, all high school subjects had reduced content, and homework was now minimally assigned in many schools. Based on research suggesting that it was unrelated to improved writing, grammar study had all but disappeared from English classes. [12] Most literary and non-literary texts with high school or college reading levels were replaced by shorter works with lower reading levels based largely on the claim that most high school literary texts in a "traditional" English curriculum were by dead white males and therefore were unappealing to a multicultural student body. In addition, it was claimed that the high school English curriculum needed to focus on "informational" texts or literary nonfiction to better prepare students for college work.

In mathematics, proofs had all but vanished from the study of geometry ("Egyptian" geometry, which focuses on shapes, was considered more useful than "Greek" geometry, which focuses on logical thinking). Euclid's *Geometry* was now a "great book," and by the twenty-first century, a weak form of Algebra I or Algebra II (not a traditional Algebra II course) emerged as the benchmark for "college readiness." The philosophical and historical antecedents of the US Constitution were gone, along with much US, English, and European history, economics, and geography. When a student in a college English class wrote about "The Rape of the Pope by Locke," only her professor could appreciate all the humor in her malapropism.

Process-oriented activities came to dominate mathematics, science, and language classes. Advanced reading in a foreign language in the upper high school grades had disappeared as speaking a foreign language on contemporary topics of daily life became the focus of the classroom. In the twenty-first century, academic content further shrank as activities addressing social and emotional learning (SEL) standards were added to each secondary subject.

Grade or Course-Title Inflation

This country was limited in its ability to judge the effect of education "reforms." High school graduation rates rose, as did the number of students who claimed on surveys that they were taking advanced courses in mathematics and science, but NAEP test scores for grade 12 students showed no changes since their inception in 1973.

Students who take AP courses in their senior year can apply to colleges in December with a transcript that shows only their enrollment in such courses, not the score from an AP exam (if they take it) because these tests are taken later in the year. Almost half the students taking AP courses now get a 1 or 2 on the exam (on a 5-point scale).[13] It is unknown what effect the many unqualified students have on qualified students in their AP classes or on discussions of the works they read. Costs to students or taxpayers are also not clear.

Links between Teacher Evaluations and Ethnicity and Student Test Scores

The beginning of the twenty-first century saw two new approaches to increase the academic status of low achievers. In the name of accountability, one approach links teacher evaluations to increases in students' test scores (the thrust of Race to the Top applications in 2010); the other approach claims that a match between students' and teachers' races or ethnicities could lead to an increase in test scores. In addition to being socially questionable, neither approach has had major effects on low achievement.[14] Nor has either approach addressed the only characteristic researchers have consistently found effective: a teacher's mastery of the subject(s) he or she teaches. Neither licensure or certification nor experience necessarily indicates subject mastery.

Public Education and the Comprehensive High School

As one education historian wrote in 2006, "education leaders effectively defended the comprehensive high school, declaring time and again that demanding . . . academic courses for all students [as the famous Committee of Ten in the 1890s wanted] would lead to a wave of dropouts and, thus, to greater education inequality."[15] According to Jeffrey Mirel, James Conant's widely cited 1959 report *The American High School Today* effectively ended the debate about the quality of American high schools for many years. In Conant's judgment, American high schools were sound, and the differentiated high school curriculum was the key to secondary schools fulfilling their democratic mission. In contrast, the Department of Education's current emphasis on workforce development for all students is controversial and has not led to widespread national and local discussions about what Americans want after grade 8 in public secondary schools: curriculum choices, a liberal arts education for all, or vocational education for all.

SUMMARY

There is no research or scholarly consensus that college readiness depends on students reading any percentage of informational texts or literary nonfiction. The myth that the English and reading curriculum should be divided between "informational texts" or "literary nonfiction" and "literature" has damaged low achievers, as well as all other students.

In order to address Common Core's English language arts standards, English teachers have had to alter their classroom curricula in ways that violate their own training. Most now teach short snippets of "informational" texts on scattered topics and few whole literary texts, except short poems.[16] In doing so, they deprive students of the opportunity to develop the academic vocabulary that grows from reading long stretches of prose in complex literary works with plots and characters to keep them reading (e.g., *Frankenstein* by Mary B. Shelley).

In few instances since 1965 was coursework for low achievers strengthened so that they ended up reading and writing at higher academic levels and showed growth on state tests. Policy makers and educators didn't know how to strengthen the school curriculum for low achievers. They did know how to flatten or lessen achievement (in other words, "kill the neighbor's cow").[17]

Because of the GI Bill and Pell Grants, postsecondary education has generally been affordable and available to all (often via "open admissions") in the large network of community colleges built across the country in the 1950s and 1960s. More than half the population has taken advantage of them. But despite grade and course-title inflation, authentic high school coursework is seen as an obstacle to college admission, not as preparation for college work.

KEY IDEAS TO REMEMBER

1. Junior high schools were an innovation at the beginning of the twentieth century, designed as a transition from nineteenth-century K–8 "grammar" schools to the new high schools built to accommodate the growing enrollment of adolescents. Compulsory education laws meant all students had to attend school until about age sixteen.

2. In grade 9 of these new high junior high schools (or in a 7–12 secondary school), four optional curriculum "tracks," or sequences of courses, were developed to encourage students who might otherwise drop out after grade 8 to continue to high school and graduate.

3. Most communities wanted just one high school for all the students who wanted a public education supported by local taxes. From this goal was born the "comprehensive American high school."

4. Teacher licensing began in the 1920s and 1930s, followed by a struggle between educators, who thought the validity of teacher licensing tests was determined by effectiveness in a classroom, and testing companies and others, who thought validity was determined by teachers' mastery of content.

5. There were many critics of the quality of public education during and immediately following World War II. Mathematics education needed to be strengthened, science education needed to be updated, and beginning reading skills needed to be taught to all students.

6. After World War II, the college track was at first strengthened, and more advanced coursework in mathematics and science was made available in our public high schools—largely to make public school students more competitive with students in nonsectarian private schools. Advanced placement courses and tests were developed for able students in any high school.

7. Congress sought to strengthen the entire K–12 curriculum with the 1958 National Defense Education Act (its response to *Sputnik* in 1957). It turned its attention away from this goal with the implementation of the Elementary and Secondary Education Act in 1965 and has consistently focused on low achievers since then. Public attention also shifted its focus to low achievers and away from the rest of the student body.

8. Middle schools (5–8) were developed after World War II to replace the junior high schools (7–9), but they inadvertently caused a change in teachers' academic qualifications for grades 7 and 8.

9. Mainly in response to teacher requests after World War II, publishers lowered the reading level of textbooks. English teachers assigned shorter and easier literary and nonliterary texts in place of the high-school-level literary and nonliterary texts they had once assigned.

10. Many schools mandated a variety of pedagogical strategies and programs to address low achievement, but none has effectively addressed low achievers.

11. The academic quality of our teacher corps continued to decline as pedagogical requirements continued to escalate. As a result, the 1993 Education Reform Act in Massachusetts requires for licensure a sub-

ject matter test and an undergraduate major in a subject taught in K–12.

12. Closing academic "gaps" between politically defined demographic groups, not a stronger curriculum for all, has become the chief mission of public education and is enforced by Congress, the Department of Education, education schools, and state departments of education. There is little local, legislative, and general public approval of this antieducational mission.

NOTES

1. Bruce Deitrick Price, "Whatever Happened to Phonics?" *American Thinker*, January 24, 2015, https://www.americanthinker.com/articles/2015/01/whatever_happened_to_phonics.html.

2. James B. Conant, *The American High School Today: A First Report to Interested Citizens* (New York: McGraw-Hill, 1957); James B. Conant, *The Comprehensive High School: A Second Report to Interested Citizens* (New York: McGraw-Hill, 1967).

3. "Cause and Purpose," K–12 Academics, 2019, https://www.k12academics.com/Federal%20Education%20Legislation/National%20Defense%20Education%20Act/cause-purpose.

4. Douglas MacIver and Allen Ruby, "Middle Schools—The Emergence of Middle Schools, Growth and Maturation of the Middle School Movement," Education Encyclopedia, 2019, http://education.stateuniversity.com/pages/2229/Middle-Schools.html.

5. For a detailed history of teacher licensing tests in this country, see Ann Jarvella Wilson, "Knowledge for Teachers: The National Teacher Examinations Program, 1940–1970," (dissertation, University of Wisconsin, 1984), University Microfilms International No. 84-14265.

6. Martha J. Bailey and Sheldon Danziger, eds., *Legacies of the War on Poverty* (New York: Russell Sage Foundation, 2013), https://www.russellsage.org/publications/legacies-war-poverty; Christopher Jencks, review of *Legacies of the War on Poverty*, edited by Martha J. Bailey and Sheldon Danziger, *New York Review of Books*, April 2, 2015, https://www.nybooks.com/articles/2015/04/02/war-poverty-was-it-lost/; Robert Rector, "How the War on Poverty Was Lost," *Daily Signal*, January 12, 2014, https://www.dailysignal.com/2014/01/12/war-poverty-lost/.

7. Joanne Weiss and Frederick Hess, "What Did Race to the Top Accomplish?" *EducationNext* 15, no. 4 (2015), https://www.educationnext.org/what-did-race-to-the-top-accomplish-forum-weiss-hess/.

8. Steven Schindler, "Measuring American Education Reform: National Assessment of Educational Progress," in *Casebook for the Foundation: A Great American Secret*, edited by Joel L. Fleishman, J. Scott Kohler, and Steven Schindler (New York: Public Affairs, 2007), 84–85, https://cspcs.sanford.duke.edu/sites/default/files/descriptive/national_assessment_of_educational_progress.pdf.

9. Philissa Cramer and Matt Barnum, "Jeff Bezos Says He Will Use His Riches to Open Montessori Preschools," Chalkbeat, September 13, 2018, https://www.chalkbeat.org/posts/us/2018/09/13/jeff-bezos-montessori-preschools/.

10. Sharon Cromwell, "Block Scheduling: A Solution or a Problem?" *Education World*, October 20, 1997, updated March 7, 2013, https://www.educationworld.com/a_admin/admin/admin029.shtml.

11. Dahlia Novarianing Asri, Punaji Setyosari, Imanuel Hitipeuw, and Tutut Chusniyah, "The Influence of Project-Based Learning Strategy and Self-Regulated Learning on Academic Procrastination of Junior High School Students' Mathematics Learning," *American Journal of Educational Research* 5, no. 1 (2017): 88–96, http://www.sciepub.com/reference/183356.

12. Beverly Ann Chin, "The Role of Grammar in Improving Student's Writing," Sadlier-Oxford, 2000, http://people.uwplatt.edu/~ciesield/graminwriting.htm.

13. Sam Dillon, "High School Classes May Be Advanced in Name Only," *New York Times*, April 26, 2011, https://www.nytimes.com/2011/04/26/education/26inflate.html.

14. Susan Aud, Mary Ann Fox, and Angelina KewalRamani, *Status and Trends in the Education of Racial and Ethnic Groups* (Washington, DC: National Center for Education Statistics, July 2010), https://nces.ed.gov/pubs2010/2010015.pdf; Kevin Mahnken, "Study: Multi-Year Gates Experiment to Improve Teacher Effectiveness Spent $575 Million, Didn't Make an Impact," *The 74*, June 21, 2018, https://www.the74million.org/study-multi-year-gates-experiment-to-improve-teacher-effectiveness-spent-575-million-didnt-make-an-impact/; Brian M. Stecher, et al., *Improving Teaching Effectiveness: Final Report: The Intensive Partnerships for Effective Teaching through 2015–2016* (Santa Monica, CA: RAND, 2018), https://www.rand.org/pubs/research_reports/RR2242.html; Madeline Will, "'An Expensive Experiment': Gates Teacher-Effectiveness Program Shows No Gains for Students," *Education Week*, December 6, 2018, https://www.edweek.org/ew/articles/2018/06/21/an-expensive-experiment-gates-teacher-effectiveness-program-show.html.

15. Jeffrey Mirel, "The Traditional High School," *EducationNext* 6, no. 1 (Winter 2006), https://www.educationnext.org/the-traditional-high-school/.

16. David Griffith and Ann Duffett, *Reading and Writing Instruction in America's Schools* (New York: Thomas Fordham Institute, 2018), https://edexcellence.net/publications/reading-and-writing-instruction-in-americas-schools.

17. Brian Stack, "Detracking Math Classrooms in San Francisco: A Model for All?" Multibriefs, July 2, 2018, http://exclusive.multibriefs.com/content/detracking-math-classrooms-in-san-francisco-a-model-for-all/education.

Chapter Two

What Policy Makers, Educators, and Education Researchers Have Examined

An extraordinary report titled *Equality of Educational Opportunity*, mandated by the Civil Rights Act of 1964, burst onto the educational scene in 1966, but its central message was distorted or forgotten almost as quickly as it was digested. Its chief author, James S. Coleman, a distinguished sociologist, and a group of colleagues spent almost two years collecting and organizing information on the many possible factors influencing academic achievement. Coleman's central observations: "All factors considered, the most important variable—in or out of school—in a child's performance remains his family's education background."[1] In addition, as a call-out in the 2016 article in *Johns Hopkins Magazine* further notes, "The conclusion that family background is far more important than people realized has remained a solid empirical finding for 50 years."[2] Indeed, the Coleman report is still the most comprehensive source of information on contextual factors affecting school achievement in this country. This chapter discusses the major finding of this report and examines major issues that educators, policy makers, and researchers spent their energies on in the several decades following its publication.

CENTRAL FINDING OF THE COLEMAN REPORT

In *EducationNext*'s 2016 commemorative issue on Coleman's report, economist and education researcher Eric Hanushek quotes its central finding:

> That schools bring little influence to bear on a child's achievement that is independent of his background and general social context; and that this very lack of an independent effect means that the inequalities imposed on children

by their home, neighborhood, and peer environment are carried along to become the inequalities with which they confront adult life at the end of school.[3]

Despite the finding that family background carries more weight than schools
and teachers in explaining academic achievement, almost all efforts to improve academic achievement in low-achieving students since then have
emerged as *educational* policies, programs, and interventions. In recent years
these initiatives have targeted all students from preschool to college, not just
low achievers.

To some extent, the focus on educational policies rather than other kinds
of policies to address low achievement is understandable. Low achievers
regardless of skin color have long been quite visible at all grade levels and in
all subjects, typically in remedial reading classes in elementary and middle
schools and in a basic curriculum sequence or track beginning in grade 9 in
comprehensive high schools and junior high schools.

Making low achievers less visible in our schools has been a major preoc-
cupation of policy makers and educators since the early 1960s; this was
usually accomplished by trying to make these students higher achievers and
eliminating remedial reading classes in elementary and middle schools and
the basic curriculum track in high school. These efforts continue to attract a
lot of public and private money, even though the initiatives to turn low
achievers into higher achievers (and sometimes to make already-high achievers into higher achievers) have been mostly ineffective—as seen in scores on
National Assessment of Educational Progress (NAEP) tests.

Educators still don't know how to turn massive numbers of low achievers
into higher achievers: High-school-level scores on NAEP tests have remained about the same for more than fifty years, but it was easier for educators and policy makers to keep telling legislators they needed more money to
implement their ideas than to explain why their ideas hadn't worked. And it
was more satisfying to legislators to award these educators more taxpayer
money than to keep nagging them and pestering noneducation "experts" for
effective ideas or explanations of failure.

In any event, Congress expected the Department of Education to handle
its appropriations in 1965 for the first authorization of the Elementary and
Secondary Education Act (ESEA), its major response to the Civil Rights Act
of 1964, and to come up with ideas to address low achievement. If Congress
understood the Coleman report, then it was unable to figure out what agency
other than an education agency could better address "family background." A
federal or state education agency could easily experiment with children compelled by law to attend school until sixteen if Congress promised money for
each state's education agency.

It was unclear, though, how the federal government could interact directly
with children who could choose when to become parents and how to parent

their own children in their own homes. The description of the early childhood initiative now being developed in Detroit and funded by the Kresge Foundation indicates that only men and women who already have children will be involved and only at the center where the services are provided. In other words, it is an educational project.

We don't know what kind of influence civil rights organizations have had on the policy approaches taken by the federal government. Did they prefer racial integration to initiatives addressing low achievement, or vice versa? They might have preferred integration, but it may not have seemed as urgent. As a result, much less was attempted than might have been if Congress heeded the central finding of the Coleman report. Instead, it chose to put most of its eggs, so to speak, in the "education" basket—the wrong basket. Moreover, Congress made a miniscule investment in the education basket to address the "inequalities imposed on children by their home, neighborhood, and peer environment."

EFFORTS TO ADDRESS THE COLEMAN REPORT

In response to the Coleman report, public officials spent their energies mainly on just one aspect of "family background": low achievers' peer environment. And they chose to do so by integrating low and higher achievers in order to achieve racial integration, thus muddying the waters. Racially segregated schools (de jure segregation) were illegal after the 1954 *Brown vs. Board of Education* Supreme Court decision. But in most parts of the country schools were racially segregated de facto because of residential patterns and zoned attendance at a neighborhood school—the closest school within walking distance for most children.

In the 1960s, some low-achieving students were able to see higher-achieving peers in the schools they attended because of state or city policies to integrate them. In most cases, this was because school attendance boundary lines had been redrawn or compulsory busing schemes had been developed to mix up different populations.[4]

Policy makers assumed that low academic achievement in black children was in large part a reflection of the influence of their peers because of racial isolation in the schools (e.g., in homogeneous remedial reading classes in middle schools or in a basic high school track). They further assumed that seeing and hearing higher (or white) achievers in their classes would motivate low (or black) achievers to work harder, even though no research suggested that this had ever happened on a small or large scale. It was insulting, to boot. What the Coleman team found were mainly correlations or relationships, not the results of experiments integrating different school populations.

Some of these attempts at school integration were successful, in that they produced no violence or rioting unlike what happened in Boston, where the integration plan was implemented in one fell swoop (not grade by grade over the years) for all public school students in kindergarten to grade 12, most of whom were from poor or working-class populations who lived in separate neighborhoods and disliked each other. But, in many cities, including Boston, these attempts led to white and black middle-class "flight" from the integrated schools and the neighborhoods surrounding the integrated schools. Unhappy parents placed their children in private schools or neighboring district schools or moved altogether.

Peaceful or not, school integration was not a panacea for low achievement, especially if compulsory busing schemes caused white students to leave the integrated schools. As many pro-busing advocates believed and said (as did James Coleman at first), if integration were to have desirable effects, then the schools being integrated needed to retain their white students.[5]

In some cities, "magnet" high schools were developed to allow high-school-age students to opt for the kind of high school coursework and specific career training they thought they wanted. Some magnet high schools were already in urban areas and sought to attract higher-achieving students from elsewhere. Some were in higher-performing areas and sought to attract low-achieving students from elsewhere. Admission could be based on a lottery, an interview, or an application. Many new vocational and regional technical high schools were also established in the 1960s and received heightened recognition and funding after various reauthorizations of the Carl D. Perkins Act through the years, with admission more likely based on an application than on winning a seat by means of a lottery.

Researchers who evaluated magnet high schools as public schools of choice came up with one of their favorite diagnoses: mixed results.[6] Over the years, some magnet high schools contributed to higher academic achievement and increased high school graduation rates for their low-income participants compared with their peers in regular high schools; others did not.[7] The extent to which magnet schools contributed to racial integration (their major purpose) and achievement is unclear, although they may have led to more racial integration and higher achievement than urban charter high schools do today.[8]

Today, magnet schools and career and technical high schools may be part of a useful array of public schools of choice in large urban districts, although they are only occasionally mentioned in discussions of school choice.[9] But career, technical, and magnet high schools have not solved the problem of massive adolescent low achievement. In fact, many magnet high schools from the outset aimed for high-achieving students because these schools tended to offer academically demanding programs at the high school level (often involving technology, science, and mathematics).[10] Their presence didn't incentivize low achievers in middle and elementary schools to work harder to qualify academically for the magnet high school of their choice.

No educational programs or strategies have yet solved the problem of massive adolescent underachievement in any major demographic groups targeted as low-income in the past fifty years.[11] According to the Coleman report, low achievement was not strongly related to the schools that low-achieving children attended, despite differences between the resources allocated to their schools and others and despite differences between the teachers they and others had. Low achievement was, as Coleman and his colleagues concluded, more a reflection of family background than their schools and teachers—then and presumably now.

That conclusion is as relevant today as it was then, even though the achievement of Hispanic immigrants today may depend heavily on generational differences in this country, their acquisition of English, and family background. Not enough attention has been paid to the spectacular academic performance of poor Asian Americans, whether immigrants, refugees, or descendants of detainees in internment camps during World War II. There is no explanation for why their educational history has been so different from the history of other demographic groups who experienced discrimination in this country. (Neither Asian Americans nor Hispanics were a large presence in this country's schools in 1965 and were not extensively studied by Coleman's team.)

WHAT EDUCATORS, RESEARCHERS, AND POLICY MAKERS FOCUSED ON INSTEAD

It is worth mentioning—however briefly—what educators, researchers, and policy makers expended their energy on in the past fifty years, even though their ideas and policies led to little or no change in the academic picture for low-achieving students and in general public education. Public and private sources have spent billions, perhaps trillions, on educational policies and other efforts to turn low achievers into higher achievers, despite the conclusion of the Coleman report that family background mattered more than schools or teachers.

Little has been spent by the federal government on the peer environments of low-achieving children—the one part of the Coleman report's conclusion that was visibly addressed. Richard Kahlenberg notes that, until the Obama administration in the 2000s provided $120 million for an initiative to support school integration, "federal support for integration consisted of a single, $100 million program for magnet schools"[12]

What have education researchers, policy makers, and educators in K–12 public schools paid attention to in their efforts to address low achievement in children from poor families?

1. Increases in Per-Pupil Spending

Many researchers have examined whether more money spent per pupil accounts for differences in achievement across school districts, even though the Coleman report notes that "variations in per-pupil expenditure had little correlation with student outcomes." This finding is noteworthy because it has been so ignored; there has been a steady drumbeat to this day for greater financing for public schools in general and for "low-income" schools in particular. [13]

Fairness alone supports the demands for roughly equal funding for all school districts, excluding teacher costs (teachers with many years of teaching experience cost more on a salary schedule than newer teachers), but expectations that providing greater funding to low-performing schools would result in higher achievement have little evidentiary grounding. While it was morally right to get rid of laws segregating students by race, it was an immoral leap of logic to expect that giving more money to a school would necessarily reduce low achievement (or to conclude that having spent more money per pupil—with no indication of what "more money" had bought—accounted for higher achievement), given the findings of the Coleman report.

Moreover, since the 1950s, schools have added teaching aides, reading and mathematics coaches, specialists, and "lead" teachers to their personnel rosters, in addition to a wide range of administrators and other personnel, such as data managers. Public schools have increasingly spent a lot of money on the biggest part of a school budget—personnel—typically, about 80 percent of education costs. As a 2017 EdChoice study on the "staffing surge" comments,

> From fiscal year (FY) 1950 to FY 2015, the earliest and most recent years with available data, American public schools added full-time equivalent (FTE) personnel at a rate almost four times that of student enrollment growth. These additional personnel were disproportionately non-teachers. While the number of FTE teachers increased almost two and a half times as fast as the increase in students—resulting in significantly smaller class sizes—the number of non-teachers or "all other staff" increased more than seven times the increase in students.
>
> . . . Despite this large investment in additional personnel, there does not seem to have been much return in terms of measured student outcomes. . . . [The staffing surge since 1992, when scores on NAEP's main tests became available] has not led to measurable academic benefits for American public school students. [14]

As the EdChoice report stresses, judging from NAEP test scores, there has been little to show for the increasing costs of K–12 education and the changes in student–teacher ratios by the end of high school. This makes it difficult to understand Hanushek's claim that the "largest impact of the Coleman Report has been in the linkage of education research to education policy."[15]

If research findings (say, from the Coleman report or from the 2008 final report by the National Mathematics Advisory Panel) have been linked to education policy, then it is not clear why the adopted policies and programs were so spectacularly ineffective. Was the research of such poor quality that it misled policy makers? The Coleman report was ignored, especially the finding that spending more money per pupil does not produce significantly higher school achievement—or its central finding—that family background explains academic achievement better than schools or teachers do.

While educators, journalists, and many others clamor for more public funds to be spent on education, it is virtually impossible to find anyone telling parents and legislators how to spend the money to make a difference to low achievers. A good example is a recent *Hechinger Report* article pointing out differences in per-pupil spending between six wealthy school districts and six poor school districts in six states.[16] The article does not explain what the wealthy school districts are spending money on to make a difference or how this can translate to low achievers in poor districts. Another example is a 2016 report by economists that finds increases in test scores when more money was allotted to low-income schools, but it does not indicate what that extra money was used for.[17]

It is equally difficult to find research supporting claims about the effectiveness of the strategies or programs in cases where the writer does indicate what we should do. See, for example, well-known educator Linda Darling-Hammond's claim:

> Over the past 30 years, a large body of research has shown that four factors consistently influence student achievement: all else equal, students perform better if they are educated in smaller schools where they are well known (300 to 500 students is optimal), have smaller class sizes (especially at the elementary level), receive a challenging curriculum, and have more highly qualified teachers.[18]

But she does not provide even one reference to support her claims, even if common sense says that most of the factors she mentions are desirable for all students, not just low achievers.

2. Measures of Teaching Effectiveness, Not Teacher Quality

Education policy makers and researchers have paid a great deal of attention to ways of measuring "teaching effectiveness," although they have tended to interpret this as teacher quality, robbing it of its essential meaning: the strength of a teacher's academic background. Economist and education researcher Dan Goldhaber asserts, "Of the characteristics [of teacher quality] that were measured in the still-revered 1966 Coleman report titled *Equality of Educational Opportunity*, those that bear the highest relationship to pupil achievement are first, the teacher's score on the verbal skills test, and then his educational background."[19]

What is noteworthy in Goldhaber's account of the Coleman report is his mention of verbal skills and educational background as two major characteristics of "teacher quality." Teacher quality does not refer to "teaching effectiveness" in a classroom—the sort of thing supposedly tapped by value-added measures (VAM), a statistical measure whose use has been heavily promoted today by a range of economists and others for assessing teacher effectiveness (and whose use has been heavily criticized, as well). Teacher quality in the Coleman report refers chiefly to what the teacher had accomplished in his or her own education, not to changes in students' test scores on nontransparent federal- or state-mandated tests (nontransparent in that parents and teachers do not ever learn who exactly vetted the test items or set the cut-off scores).

Race to the Top (RttT) was a grant competition from the Obama administration in 2010 to encourage states to develop teacher evaluation plans related in some way to student scores on tests aligned with Common Core's standards. However, RttT did not encourage states to hire new teachers with stronger verbal skills and academic majors than their experienced teachers had or reward states for doing so.

The template for the accountability or "state plan" built into the December 2015 reauthorization of the Elementary and Secondary Education Act, called Every Student Succeeds Act (ESSA), also did not require states or school districts to commit to hiring new teachers with stronger verbal skills and stronger academic majors. ESSA asked mainly for licensed or "certified" teachers—a bow to the education schools.

Yet, the research relating teacher characteristics to student achievement has been consistent and clear and mostly corroborates Coleman's 1966 findings. The task group on teachers and teacher education for the National Mathematics Advisory Panel notes that the chief teacher characteristic related to student achievement, according to the well-designed research it reviewed (using criteria spelled out in advance), was teachers' knowledge of the subject(s) they taught.[20]

Confusion about the meaning of teacher quality abounds in the research. Roland Fryer, another prominent economist, uses "excellence in teaching" as a possible synonym for teacher quality in the school improvement program he helped to design in 2010 for Houston, Texas.[21] He did *not* find a relationship between student scores and teachers with certification or an advanced degree, but he does not explain why a teaching license should necessarily have ever meant that a teacher with a state-awarded license was better than a teacher without one. Many highly regarded private schools—both sectarian and nonsectarian—to this day do not have to hire state-licensed teachers, and many traditionally have avoided hiring state-licensed teachers.

Fryer also does not explain what he means by an "advanced degree." One cannot infer that an MEd holder, for example, knows more about anything (including pedagogy) than someone without an MEd. In contrast, an MAT degree program was an attempt to remedy that situation (half the coursework was in graduate work in the field of the license; the other half, in related pedagogy), but there are few such programs today for training teachers. If there were, then we might not have the crisis we are developing. A large number of prospective teachers fail their state licensure tests, all developed to ensure that children are protected from academically incompetent teachers.

Education schools blame the tests, not their own admission procedures and preparation programs, for these failure rates. What is worse, reporters are just as eager to consider the tests as a problem, not a necessity. (Common Core–aligned tests for K–12 students are often rationalized as necessary; otherwise, we are told, we would not know who the weak students are.)

As reported in February 2017, "In 2015, the state of Florida revised its teacher licensing exam to better reflect changes already made to standardized tests for students." In fact, many aspiring teachers have failed that exam: "At the University of South Florida, last year more than 10% of students were impacted by their failure to pass the state-mandated teacher test, or FTCE. Included in that 10% were about 70 students who graduated with a diploma but not a passing score on the state's test."[22] Remarkably, there was no observation that, without that state-mandated teacher test, K–12 students might otherwise have been taught by academically unqualified teachers.

Another case in point is North Carolina. In 2017, the discrepancy between expectation and performance came to public attention in a newspaper article in the *Charlotte Observer* on the large number of prospective elementary and special education teachers failing a required elementary mathematics test for licensure.[23] The supposed problem with the test is magnified to the national level by an article in *Newsweek*, but this still does not provide an accurate description of the test. An August 2018 article, again in the *Charlotte Observer*, finally raises the question of teacher preparation but suggests that the test was wrong because it was not about primary-grade pedagogy.[24] However, the test was not intended to be about primary-grade pedagogy but about the mathematical competence of the test takers—prospective teachers. The basic issue raised implicitly by the story was *not* why the test (used in Massachusetts with the same results) was *not* the problem but why many prospective elementary and special education teachers in North Carolina, most of whom had graduated from North Carolina high schools and colleges, were mathematically deficient.

Were low scores on NAEP tests in mathematics a result of the influence of academically unqualified teachers on the state's children? And were teachers' deficiencies a reflection of the coursework they had taken in high school aligned to "college readiness" standards and tests? Or did they reflect a lack of preparation (no required elementary mathematics courses) in teacher-preparation programs?

A report issued by the state board of education in August 2018 doesn't tell how its education schools are preparing prospective elementary teachers in mathematics. Were they required to take courses in elementary mathematics, as well as in mathematics education, or just methods coursework?[25] The report also does not explain the mathematics coursework these prospective teachers had taken in high school, even if they had been deemed "college-ready" as high school students. The report's authors decided at the outset that the test was guilty.

In Massachusetts, the introduction of the same elementary mathematics licensure test in 2009 (North Carolina adopted the Bay State test and simply changed its name) was preceded by advice to all elementary-teacher-preparation programs in 2007 on the coursework in mathematics (not mathematics education) all prospective elementary teachers should have in their preparation programs (namely, two to three courses in elementary mathematics).[26] The testing company also provided a lengthy practice test.

No information is available from either state on (1) whether all prospective teachers required to take this licensure test were in programs that prepared them for teaching mathematics from grades 1 to 6 (the scope of the license) and (2) how they were prepared, if at all. In any event, the Bay State is the only state where 50 percent of its children reach "proficient" on both NAEP mathematics and reading tests in grades 4 and 8.[27] A state, then, should already know the content its students learned in K–12 and college before they are admitted into its elementary-teacher-preparation programs.

3. Pedagogy for Skills, Strategies, and Processes

Education policy makers and researchers have paid extraordinary attention to the skills, strategies, and processes used in teaching or learning the subjects in the school curriculum but not to their basic content, for many reasons. The major reason may be that basic academic content (i.e., the school curriculum) and instruction are constitutionally the province of the local community. The result of the inordinate attention to skills, strategies, and processes was a reduction in the disciplinary content taught to most students mainly because there was less time for teaching it. How so?

Most state-developed standards from the 1990s on, as well as the Gates Foundation–funded standards (Common Core's standards in English language arts and mathematics, adopted by most states by 2011), claimed to address only the standards for the K–12 curriculum, not how to teach its content. Yet, most pre–Common Core standards, as well as Common Core's standards themselves, required the use of specific skills, strategies, or processes in English language arts, mathematics, and other subjects.

By requiring teachers and students to pay more attention (often much more) to, for example, the "writing process," the "reading process," or the "scientific method" than they had previously, time for teaching basic content was inevitably lessened. There *is* a "process" in most, if not all, subjects that needs to be taught, but not at the expense of the basic knowledge that the process draws on. There *are* thinking skills to be developed in every subject in K–12 but not at the expense of the basic knowledge that becomes the basis for thoughts.

Mandates for teaching processes, strategies, or skills may be given directly in a standards document in introductory matter or in the form of regular "standards" or as part of its standards. It's hard to find a pre–Common Core set of state writing standards that did not require the "writing process" (brainstorming, drafting, revising, editing, etc.) in the form of standards to be taught at all grade levels. Many sets of science standards in this country today require students to learn the "scientific process" or "scientific method" (hypothesizing, designing an experiment, observing, etc.) in the form of standards taught at all grade levels. Common Core set forth "literacy" standards for use in all subjects, but we don't know how much time has been taken away from content learning in, say, mathematics, science, and history.

4. Ways to Distort or Omit Academic Content

While education policy makers have paid inordinate attention to processes, strategies, and skills in the past fifty years, they have paid little or no attention to the content itself and to the distinction between content and pedagogy. The absence of attention to this problem has often resulted in a distortion of the basic K–12 curriculum because it has affected the way in which a standards document is organized at its top level. For example, the first draft (in 1995) of the Bay State's later-lauded English language arts standards featured organizing strands (ways to cluster standards in an area) on "strategies" and "discussion." For the first revision of this draft, a new standards development committee immediately replaced pedagogy ("strategies" and "discussion") with academic content (e.g., history of the English language).

As another example, to address Common Core's English language arts standards, English teachers have been told to increase the amount of "informational text" they teach. The Core's lead writers attribute this "special emphasis" to NAEP reading assessments, despite the warning in NAEP's own assessment materials that NAEP does not "prescribe a particular curricular approach." This distortion of the high school English curriculum is reinforced by Common Core's division of reading into a roughly equal number of standards for literature and informational text.

Literary nonfiction has long accounted for about 20 percent of English teachers' reading instructional time—in the form of speeches, essays, biographies, and autobiographies (the other 80 percent is devoted to fiction, drama, and poetry). But after 2010 and the adoption of the Gates-funded Core standards by most states, English teachers were told to teach "informational texts" for well over half of their reading instructional time. There is no research that justifies an equal division of reading and literature standards in the secondary grades into two major types of reading material, nor is there evidence to support an overemphasis on "literary nonfiction" in the form of "informational text."

In mathematics, something similar took place decades ago. According to most mathematics standards documents, K–12 teachers were expected to spend much instructional time on a strand called "data analysis, statistics, and probability." It came to consume a great deal of time in the mathematics curriculum once teachers knew that the strand and the standards in that area would be covered on a mandated test.

Mathematics education policy makers today also expect many "strategies" to be taught as part of mathematics standards. For example, in a grade 3 Common Core mathematics standard, students are asked to "multiply one-digit whole numbers by multiples of 10 in the range 10–90 (e.g., 9×80, 5×60) using strategies based on place value and properties of operations." That grade 3 standard mandates pedagogy ("using strategies"). It does not ask for the use of the standard multiplication algorithm, which might, ironically in this case, be considered content knowledge. Basic content was reduced and displaced when the basic curriculum was distorted for the organizing framework for a set of standards. Mathematical "strategies" in the primary grades for basic arithmetical operations in effect became standards.

Let's look now at the high school level in English, where the greatest damage has been done, not just to the English curriculum, but also to the entire school curriculum. Education policy makers, curriculum specialists, and researchers have tended in recent decades to pay little attention to the real content of the high school English class. That content always consisted of the specific literary works assigned to all students for reading, discussion, and analysis. Perhaps English curriculum supervisors hoped to avoid controversies about teachers' literary and nonliterary choices or their reading levels by not arguing for more specific curricular guidelines (such as literary periods, movements, traditions, recommended authors) to accompany current high school reading and literature standards. Nevertheless, there is a huge hole in the curriculum where critical (analytical) skills were once developed. And there is not one state that requires its students to become familiar with the well-known essays, speeches, or writers who lived in or wrote about their state or region (e.g., Oklahoma's standards do not expect students to become familiar with Will Rogers).

The literary content of the high school English class has been ignored or turned into snippets (excerpts). The last two surveys of the whole works that high school English teachers have assigned (pre–Common Core, so to speak) were done by Arthur Applebee in 1990 and Sandra Stotsky, Joan Traffas, and James Woodworth in 2010, but there have been no others since then.[28]

One may speculate that it has been much easier for educators and others to make claims about what English teachers teach as reading skills because, in a standards-based environment, they tend to be about the same from grade to grade, even if paraphrased differently to avoid repetition. For example, a grade 7 skill-oriented "literature" standard in Common Core's English language arts standards document states, "Cite several pieces of textual evidence to support analysis of what the text says explicitly as well as inferences drawn from the text. (CCSS.ELA-LITERACY. RI.7.1)." The same standard for grades 9–10 in the same document states, "Cite strong and thorough textual evidence to support analysis of what the text says explicitly as well as inferences drawn from the text (CCSS.ELA-LITERACY. RI.9–10.1)." Not much difference between these two "standards," although they are at very different grade levels!

There should be little confusion between skills, strategies, and processes as standards and real content standards. Skills typically contain nothing of cultural content or level of reading difficulty. An empty, culture-free skill (as in the previous examples) can apply equally to the "Three Little Pigs" or *Moby-Dick*. In contrast, a content standard may refer to discipline-based knowledge (e.g., a specific work's influence or its literary period or movement), cultural knowledge, an appropriate reading level for a particular grade, or any combination of these. As an example, a pre–Common Core standard for English language arts in Massachusetts for grades 9–10 expected students to identify the theme and structural elements of classical Greek or Roman epic poetry. English teachers in the Bay State at the time (around 2001) recommended the standard and knew that the curricular possibilities included their choice of *The Iliad*, *The Odyssey*, or *The Aeneid*—all appropriate for most ninth- or tenth-graders in the state at that time.

Grade-less skills are no substitute for intellectual standards. Nevertheless, standards in the form of skills are popular with test developers and curriculum specialists because they can be stretched to fit most grade levels. They facilitate development of test items for a specific subject or a reading curriculum for different grade levels because one doesn't have to spend a lot of time determining the content suitable for the grade-level of the test or a sequence for the cumulative learning of the content that, in fact, develops the skills.

However, meaningful (coherent) content sequences at different reading levels (for different grade levels) are major issues in curriculum development because such sequences are related to the vocabulary and paragraph density needed for the content of specific subjects at specific grade levels. Decisions on the level of vocabulary and paragraph density to use were once made in-house by school textbook publishers. But it's rare for this to be done in a careful, methodical way today when teachers can easily pull unrelated lessons off a website (or are encouraged to do so) and compile their own idiosyncratic textbooks and anthologies.

Even when a school provides its English teachers with an anthology to use, they are now so bulky (to address every possible literary need) that a majority of high school English teachers in grades 9, 10, and 11 claim they use fewer than half of the selections in them.[29] The K–12 curriculum has been seriously wounded by skills, strategies, and processes as standards and by distorted curricula,[30] but no one has documented what happened over time in even one school district. States were incentivized by RttT funds to adopt skills as standards in reading and other language arts (called college- and career-ready standards), and student learning has deteriorated at a national level in part as a result of this adoption.

Aside from the curriculum sequences for all subjects spelled out in the Core Knowledge Curriculum (issued by the Core Knowledge Foundation in Charlottesville, Virginia), in mathematics in the original Singapore Math program for K–6, and in the K–6 literature readers created for the Open Court reading and language arts program of the mid-1990s, there has been little serious intellectual work on the content of the K–12 curriculum since the *Sputnik* era more than fifty years ago. The academic work on revising and modernizing curriculum content, especially in mathematics and science, by means of grants to participants at National Defense Education Act (NDEA) institutes during the 1950s and 1960s just about ceased after passage of ESEA in 1965.

Congress established the National Assessment Governing Board (NAGB) in 1988 to govern policies for NAEP testing, which began in the late 1960s as the Nation's Report Cards and as a response to the alarming drop in SAT verbal and math scores in 1963. In 1992, under NAGB's auspices, NAEP began a new series of tests, called the main tests—to reflect major changes in pedagogy but continued giving the original tests as long-term trend tests. As of 2018, these tests have been suspended by NAGB until the mid-2020s, supposedly for budgetary reasons, leaving this country without a way to find out what has happened nationwide to the level of education in its schools.

A few brave literary souls have tried to arouse attention to the reading curriculum for all students (e.g., James Moffett in the 1960s and E. D. Hirsch in the 1980s), but their basic ideas didn't make serious inroads into the practices of education schools and most educators. Educators' shared goal was no longer strengthening public education (a goal after World War II, largely in response to criticisms by Admiral Hyman Rickover, historian Arthur Bestor, and a few other well-known critics). The ostensible goal was to enable more students to graduate from public high schools and enroll in postsecondary institutions with greater knowledge and skills. In practice, it led to the shrinking of content.

The downgrading of curriculum content, especially in the reading curriculum from 1970 on, was accompanied by (perhaps caused in large part by) an increasing emphasis on pedagogy in teacher licensure tests in all subjects instead of knowledge of subject matter.[31] The overall goal may have been justified as fairness to lower-achieving prospective teachers and as the best way to assert the importance of pedagogy itself. But it also meant that all students would learn less content because most licensure tests didn't expect elementary teachers (or any K–8 teachers) to know much about the subjects they taught.

5. Size of the Schools Attended by Low Achievers and School Schedules

Some attention has been paid to the size of our high schools, especially in the 2000s, when American high schools were suddenly declared obsolete.[32] They were too large, we were told. What was strikingly absent from such declarations was evidence that size was a systemic problem independent of the student body in a high school—or that the difficulty large numbers of students have had in doing high-school-level work is a function of the size of their school.

It is true that many large urban high schools have a low-achieving student body. But large urban high schools with a high-achieving student body have had relatively few dropouts and seemingly few complaints by parents, teachers, or students about their size. For example, in 2004–2005, at about the time large high schools were declared obsolete, examination schools in New York City (now called "specialized" schools) ranged from Bronx High School of Science, with 2,617 students, and Stuyvesant High School, with 3,059 students, to Brooklyn Technical High School, with 4,062 students, with similar numbers at other very high-performing (but not examination) high schools, such as Benjamin Cardozo High School, with 3,972 students, and James Madison High School, with 3,978 students. New York City parents and students clearly did not think all large high schools were dysfunctional. In 2005 almost 30,000 students took the entrance test for the fewer than 8,000 available seats in the examination schools. The numbers in

2013–2014 at the older exam schools in New York City were about as high, if not higher.[33]

Since the Gates Foundation stopped funding "small schools" initiatives (mostly high schools and mostly in the New York City area), there have been fewer attempts at smaller high schools and less research on them. That is unfortunate because there may well be too many small high schools in rural areas.

The last systematic look at the American high school took place during and right after World War II, at a time when many American students attended public high schools that were *too small*. For two landmark reports, *The American High School Today* and *The Comprehensive High School*, a team of educators led by James B. Conant, longtime president of Harvard University and a former chemistry professor, used a long list of specific criteria for judging the adequacy of a high school's curriculum at a time when test data on student outcomes were unavailable.[34] Criteria ranged from instruction in calculus to courses for slow learners.

Based on visits to or surveys of hundreds of schools, Conant and his team of educators conclude that an "excellent comprehensive high school can be developed in any school district provided the high school enrolls at least 750 students and sufficient funds are available."[35] Consolidation of small high schools into a regional high school was one way to achieve this number, and it took place in many states.

Conant suggests that academically motivated students benefit from high schools that can offer honors and advanced placement courses and a four-year sequence in at least two foreign languages. He also suggests that larger high schools could also benefit students with learning disabilities or underachieving students who are potential dropouts by providing the intensive help with reading and mathematics these students need, as well as a choice of career-oriented curricula and academic coursework at their levels of skill.

One of Conant's purposes in consolidating public high schools in this country was to get more qualified students from public high schools into Ivy League colleges. Up to and through World War II, the bulk of the students at our most demanding liberal arts colleges came from private schools. He wanted stronger coursework available in public high schools for any student motivated to take it, and he wanted stronger teachers in our public high schools—in mathematics and science, in particular. Small public high schools do not tend to offer strong coursework in mathematics or science.

But instead of a more careful look at school size, researchers today look at the school schedule to see if the starting time should be changed to accommodate adolescents' sleep schedules better and if the school schedule itself should be changed to allow teachers more planning time.[36] Many studies have looked at block scheduling to see if students gained from different ways of organizing class time. Generally, researchers have not found enough evidence to recommend block scheduling as a way to improve academic achievement. In fact, many studies have found it detrimental or damaging. Researchers at the University of London should be congratulated for looking at both issues.[37]

6. Low-Achieving Schools: The Search for an Effective Turnaround Model

Much time and money has been spent by the Department of Education, states, and local districts in efforts to "transform" low-achieving schools into higher-achieving schools. The idea for turnaround schools began as part of No Child Left Behind (NCLB), the reauthorization of ESEA under President Bush in 2001. The turnaround policy was one of four choices suggested by the Bush administration (but mandated by the Obama administration) for schools that didn't meet adequate yearly progress (AYP) for a number of years and could be judged as "chronically low-performing."

Most, if not all, schools designated as turnaround schools did not turn student achievement around. Low-performing schools, for the most part, remained low-performing schools, despite the amount of money the federal government sent to state departments of education to turn them around. From 2002 to about 2008, more than four billion dollars was sent to state departments of education, chiefly in the form of school improvement grants (SIGs).[38]

The Department of Education did ask for an examination of state capacity for turnaround[39] and found out, not surprisingly, that states needed more money for more consultant expertise for this kind of work. It didn't find out how much these various "intermediaries" received from whatever work they did with low-performing schools or even how many low-performing schools in each state were able to move out of the category in which they had been placed with the help of the "intermediaries" they had partnered with. It was a given that these "intermediaries" (all categorically listed on page 8 of the report to the Department of Education) had the expertise for turning around low-performing schools. However, it was widely recognized that state departments of education did not have the capacity for addressing all the problems in public schools and that the purpose of most of this federal money was to enable state education agencies to partner with available "experts."[40]

To make matters worse, one can also infer from the report that the federal government was likely trying to blame the states for the failure of turnaround schools to improve student achievement. Never had the Department of Education sought an evaluation of the turnaround *partners* that states and schools were often coerced into using. Nor in the research on turnaround is there a hint that the policy itself may not be a wise one. This possibility is suggested by the

absence of such a discussion in the collection of essays on the topic published by
the National Association of State Boards of Education (NASBE).[41]

7. A Variety of Curricular and Staffing
Policies and Programs for K–12

Many changes in the school curriculum for all students or programs to improve the academic performance of low achievers took place. These policies
and programs included changes in approaches to beginning reading, such as a
"whole language" or "guessing game" approach; preschool programs for
low-income three- and four-year-olds; changes in the content of the K–12
reading and literature curriculum, often in the name of multiculturalism;
professional development programs for teachers and administrators; home
visits; smaller classes in the primary grades; longer school days or years;
test-based retention in grade 3 for low achievers; increases in nonteaching
personnel; mathematics and reading coaches in K–8; changes in teaching
mathematics and reading; and standards-based classroom curricula, tests, and
professional development.[42] Evaluations of the totality of these efforts show
little, if any, meaningful improvement for low achievers on a nationwide
basis. Community or full-service schools have also been tried out, but they
haven't been in existence long enough for judgment of academic and cost
effectiveness.

SUMMARY

The failure of all the efforts to turn massive numbers of low-achieving minority students into higher achievers since 1966 has raised a basic unanswered question: Why were the schools—or our educational institutions in
general—bearing the brunt of these efforts?[43] For example, Leah Gordon
writes, "Why educational approaches to fighting poverty and inequality have
persistently generated so much enthusiasm, even in moments—and the Coleman Report certainly generated one of them—when schooling's limits as an
egalitarian lever were as squarely in view as its potential, remains a pressing
question for historians and advocates of social justice alike."[44]

She doesn't mention what happened (or didn't happen) in Kansas City in
the late 1980s and early 1990s, after a judge ordered more money for the
integration of its schools than educators could spend. Achievement still
didn't rise for minority kids. Although a CATO report on the Kansas City
Desegregation Experiment (as it was called) came out in 1998, no educators
have mentioned the obvious lesson that came out of the Kansas City experiment: Low achievement may not be addressable by educators or educational
institutions.[45]

KEY IDEAS TO REMEMBER

1. The central finding of the 1966 Coleman report is that family background carries more weight than schools and teachers in explaining academic achievement.
2. Despite this finding, most efforts and funds to help low achievers from low-income families have targeted their schools.
3. Researchers and education policy makers in the past half-century have paid much attention to the following areas (among others): (1) increased per-pupil spending, (2) teacher accountability measures, (3) pedagogy for skills and processes, (4) distorting or omitting content knowledge, (5) the size of the schools attended by low achievers and the school schedule, (6) turning around low-achieving schools via turnaround models, and (7) a range of curricular and staffing policies and programs for K–12.
4. Evaluations of efforts in these areas have shown little, if any, meaningful improvement for low achievers nationally on a consistent basis.
5. Community or full-service schools haven't been in existence long enough for informed judgments of long-term academic gains and cost effectiveness.
6. Results of the Kansas City experiment in the 1980s and 1990s raised the still-unanswered question, Is massive low achievement addressable by educators or educational institutions?

NOTES

1. Elizabeth Evitts Dickinson, "Coleman Report Set the Standard for the Study of Public Education," *Johns Hopkins Magazine* (Winter 2016), https://hub.jhu.edu/magazine/2016/winter/coleman-report-public-education/.

2. Dickinson, "Coleman Report Set the Standard."

3. Eric Hanushek, "What Matters for Student Achievement—Updating Coleman on the Influence of Families and Schools," *EducationNext* 16, no. 2 (Spring 2016), http://educationnext.org/what-matters-for-student-achievement/.

4. Wikipedia Contributors, "Desegregation Busing," *Wikipedia*, accessed December 6, 2018, https://en.wikipedia.org/w/index.php?title=Desegregation_busing&oldid=871500195.

5. Diane Ravitch, "Busing: The Solution That Has Failed to Solve," *New York Times*, December 21, 1975, 117, https://www.nytimes.com/1975/12/21/archives/busing-the-solution-that-has-failed-to-solve.html.

6. Grace Chen, "What Is a Magnet School?" *Public School Review*, updated June 22, 2017, https://www.publicschoolreview.com/blog/what-is-a-magnet-school; "A Review of the Research on Magnet Schools," Information Capsule, January 2012, http://magnet.edu/research-category/magnet-school-research.

7. Adam Gamoran, "Do Magnet Schools Boost Achievement?" *Educational Leadership* 54, no. 2 (October 1996): 42–46, http://www.ascd.org/publications/educational-leadership/oct96/vol54/num02/Do-Magnet-Schools-Boost-Achievement%C2%A2.aspx.

8. Julian Betts, Sami Kitmitto, Jesse Levin, Johannes Bos, and Marian Eaton, *What Happens When Schools Become Magnet Schools? A Longitudinal Study of Diversity and Achievement* (Washington, DC: American Institutes for Research, May 2015), https://www.air.org/

resource/what-happens-when-schools-become-magnet-schools-longitudinal-study-diversity-and.

9. Magnet schools are mentioned as one of the choices parents have by EdChoice at https://www.edchoice.org/school-choice/types-of-school-choice.

10. Crystal Lombardo, "Pros and Cons of Magnet Schools," Vision Launch, September 10, 2015, http://visionlaunch.com/pros-and-cons-of-magnet-schools.

11. Sandra Stotsky, *Changing the Course of Failure: How Schools and Parents Can Help Low-Achieving Students* (Lanham, MD: Rowman & Littlefield, 2018).

12. Richard D. Kahlenberg, "School Integration's Comeback," *Atlantic*, February 10, 2016, https://www.theatlantic.com/education/archive/2016/02/breaking-up-school-poverty/462066.

13. See, for example, Bruce D. Baker, *Does Money Matter in Education?* 2nd ed. (Washington, DC: Albert Shanker Institute, 2016), http://www.shankerinstitute.org/resource/does-money-matter-second-edition.

14. Benjamin Scafidi, *Back to the Staffing Surge: The Great Teacher Salary Stagnation and the Decades-Long Employment Growth in American Public Education* (Indianapolis: EdChoice, May 2017), https://www.edchoice.org/wp-content/uploads/2017/05/Back-to-the-Staffing-Surge-by-Ben-Scafidi.pdf.

15. Hanushek, "What Matters for Student Achievement."

16. Jill Barshay, "In 6 States, School Districts with the Neediest Students Get Less Money than the Wealthiest," *Hechinger Report*, July 9, 2018, https://hechingerreport.org/in-6-states-school-districts-with-the-neediest-students-get-less-money-than-the-wealthiest.

17. Julien Lafortune, Jesse Rothstein, and Diane Whitmore Schanzenbach, "School Finance Reform and the Distribution of Student Achievement," National Bureau of Economic Research Working Paper No. 22011, February 2016, https://www.nber.org/papers/w22011.pdf.

18. Linda Darling-Hammond, "Unequal Opportunity: Race and Education," *Brookings Review*, March 1, 1998, https://www.brookings.edu/articles/unequal-opportunity-race-and-education.

19. Dan Goldhaber, "In Schools, Teacher Quality Matters Most—Today's Research Reinforces Coleman's Findings," *EducationNext* 16, no. 2 (Spring 2016), http://educationnext.org/in-schools-teacher-quality-matters-most-coleman.

20. Deborah Loewenberg Ball, James Simons, Hung-Hsi Wu, Raymond Simon, Grover J. "Russ" Whitehurst, and Jim Yun, "Chapter 5: Report of the Task Group on Teachers and Teacher Education," in *Foundations for Success: The Final Report of the National Mathematics Advisory Panel* (Washington, DC: US Department of Education, 2008), 5–7, https://www2.ed.gov/about/bdscomm/list/mathpanel/report/teachers.pdf; National Mathematics Advisory Panel, *Foundations for Success: The Final Report of the National Mathematics Advisory Panel* (Washington, DC: US Department of Education, 2008), https://www2.ed.gov/about/bdscomm/list/mathpanel/report/final-report.pdf.

21. For Fryer's account of the Houston program and its results, see Roland G. Fryer Jr., "Injecting Successful Charter School Strategies into Traditional Public Schools: A Field Experiment in Houston," National Bureau of Economic Research Working Paper No. 1749, revised December 12, 2013, http://www.nber.org/papers/w17494.

22. Katie Lagrone and Matthew Apthorp, "More Teachers Are Failing State-Mandated FTCE, Florida Teacher Certification Exam," *WFTS Tampa Bay*, February 3, 2017, https://www.abcactionnews.com/longform/teachers-failing-state-certification-test-at-alarming-rates.

23. Ann Doss Helms, "Could You Pass This Math Test? Hundreds of NC Teachers Have Failed It," *Charlotte Observer*, August 9, 2018, https://www.charlotteobserver.com/news/local/education/article216196615.html; Ann Doss Helms, "Hundreds of NC Teachers Are Flunking Math Exam. It May Not Be Their Fault," *Charlotte Observer*, August 2, 2018, https://www.charlotteobserver.com/news/local/education/article215848065.html.

24. Ann Doss Helms, "As Math Test Denies NC Teachers Licenses, Hundreds of Classrooms Remain Unstaffed," *Charlotte Observer*, August 10, 2018, https://www.charlotteobserver.com/news/local/education/article216246840.html.

25. Thomas Tomberlin and Andrew Sioberg, *Educator Preparation and Licensure Exams*, North Carolina State Board of Education, August 2018.

26. Tom Fortmann, *Guidelines for the Mathematical Preparation of Elementary Teachers* (Malden: Massachusetts Department of Education, July 2007), http://www.doe.mass.edu/mtel/MathGuidance.pdf.

27. Massachusetts Department of Education, "Massachusetts NAEP Results Lead Nation for 12th Year," Mass.gov, April 10, 2018, https://www.mass.gov/news/massachusetts-naep-results-lead-nation-for-12th-year.

28. Arthur N. Applebee, "Book-Length Works Taught in High School English Courses," ERIC Clearinghouse on Reading and Communication Skills, May 1990, ED318035; Sandra Stotsky, Joan Traffas, and James Woodworth, "Literary Study in Grades 9, 10, and 11: A National Survey," *Forum* 4 (Fall 2010), http://alscw.org/wp-content/uploads/2017/04/forum_4.pdf.

29. Sandra Stotsky, Christian Goering, and David Jolliffe, "Literary Study in Grades 9, 10, and 11 in Arkansas" (unpublished report, University of Arkansas, 2009), https://cied.uark.edu/_resources/pdf/literary-study-czg.pdf; Stotsky, Traffas, and Woodworth, "Literary Study."

30. Maggie Lit, "The Average College Freshman Reads at 7th Grade Level," *Campus Reform*, January 6, 2015, https://www.campusreform.org/?ID=6174; Sandra Stotsky, "What Bay State Teachers Should Do about Our High School Reading Problem," *New Boston Post*, June 8, 2016, http://newbostonpost.com/blogs/what-bay-state-teachers-should-do-about-our-high-school-reading-problem.

31. See chapter 4 in Sandra Stotsky, *An Empty Curriculum* (Lanham, MD: Rowman & Littlefield, 2015), for details on the evolution of the content of teacher licensure tests in the twentieth century and the number of testing hours.

32. Paul Hill, "A Foundation Goes to School: Bill and Melinda Gates Shift from Computers in Libraries to Reform in High Schools," *EducationNext* 6, no. 1 (Winter 2006), https://www.educationnext.org/afoundationgoestoschool.

33. "Best High Schools: See New York's Top 60 Institutions, from the Bronx to Staten Island," *New York Daily News*, October 15, 2014, http://www.nydailynews.com/new-york/education/best-high-schools-new-york-top-60-institutions-article-1.1973796.

34. James B. Conant, *The American High School Today* (New York: McGraw-Hill, 1957); James B. Conant, *The Comprehensive High School* (New York: McGraw-Hill, 1967).

35. Conant, *Comprehensive High School*, 2.

36. Brenda Iasevoli, "It's Time to Rethink School Schedules, Report Says," *Teacher Beat*, February 27, 2017, http://blogs.edweek.org/edweek/teacherbeat/2017/02/report_its_time_to_rethink_sch.html?intc=main-mpsmvs.

37. Kelly Dickson, Karen Bird, Mark Newman, and Naira Kalra, "What Is the Effect of Block Scheduling on Academic Achievement? A Systematic Review. Technical Report," in *Research Evidence in Education Library* (London: EPPI-Centre, Social Science Research Unit, Institute of Education, University of London, 2010), http://eppi.ioe.ac.uk/cms/Default.aspx?tabid=2476.

38. Sandra Stotsky and Trae Holzman, "The Costs of Federal Intervention in Local Education: The Effectiveness of America's Choice in Arkansas," *Nonpartisan Education Review* 11, no. 2 (2015): 1–16, https://nonpartisaneducation.org/Review/Articles/v11n2.pdf.

39. "State Capacity to Support School Turnaround," NCEE Evaluation Brief, May 2015, https://ies.ed.gov/ncee/pubs/20154012/pdf/20154012.pdf; Sandra Stotsky, "Government Sponsored Research on Education: The Evaluation Brief on State Capacity for 'Turnaround,'" *Education News*, May 10, 2015, http://www.educationviews.org/government-sponsored-research-education-evaluation-state-capacity-turnaround.

40. Lindsey Layton, "Most States Lacked Expertise to Improve Worst Schools," *Washington Post*, May 5, 2015, https://www.washingtonpost.com/local/education/most-states-lacked-expertise-to-improve-worst-schools/2015/05/05/0eb82b98-f35f-11e4-bcc4-e8141e5eb0c9_story.html?utm_term=.6511bee594a5.

41. Carlas McCauley, "A Systems Approach to Rapid School Improvement," *Standard* 18, no. 2 (May 2018): 6–9, 46–47, http://www.nasbe.org/wp-content/uploads/2018/05/McCauley_May-2018-Standard.pdf.

42. See chapter 5 in Stotsky, *Changing the Course*.

43. Leah Gordon, "The Coleman Report and Its Critics: The Contested Meanings of Educational Equality in the 1960s and 1970s," *Process: A Blog for American History*, March 22, 2017, http://www.processhistory.org/gordon-coleman-report.

44. Gordon, "Coleman Report and Its Critics."

45. Paul Ciotti, "Money and School Performance: Lessons from the Kansas City Desegregation Experiment," *Policy Analysis*, no. 298, March 16, 1998, https://www.cato.org/publications/policy-analysis/money-school-performance-lessons-kansas-city-desegregation-experiment.

Chapter Three

Teachers of Minority Students in 1966

This chapter discusses what Coleman's team found when it compared the characteristics of the teachers of minority and nonminority children. Did the teachers of minority children differ from the teachers of nonminority children in significant ways? If so, how? Needless to say, important differences were found, yet Congress has done little to follow up on what the Coleman team found. Education policy makers did little after 1966 to address "teacher quality," even though it was, as Coleman and his team wrote, "one of the few school characteristics that significantly affects student performance."

WHAT THE COLEMAN REPORT FOUND ABOUT TEACHERS OF MINORITY CHILDREN

The Coleman report highlights the differences it found between the teachers of "white" children and the teachers of "Negro" children based on the information Coleman's team collected from schools across the country. Their diagnosis: "We have seen in earlier sections that the teachers of white children differ from the teachers of Negro children in average verbal skills, that Negro teachers typically teach Negro students, and that teacher quality is one of the few school characteristics that significantly affects student performance."[1]

The implication of that sentence should be clear to all. If anything should have been a red flag to policy makers to focus on the quality of the teaching force in schools with large numbers of minority children, that sentence alone would have been the signal. It could easily have served as the basis for state policies to strengthen admission and exiting requirements in teacher-preparation programs—for the teachers of all students, white and black. The federal government could have persistently and consistently encouraged such policies before leaving teacher training and licensure alone since because they were and remain responsibilities of state governments. Instead, the signal was ignored.

THE CONTEXT FOR THE COLEMAN
REPORT'S FINDINGS ON TEACHERS

The Coleman report came out more than a decade after the *Brown vs. Board of Education* decision by the US Supreme Court in 1954 and only a few years after the scores for the SAT verbal and mathematics tests plunged in 1963. It should have been clear a year after Congress's first authorization of the Elementary and Secondary Education Act (ESEA) in 1965 that paying serious attention to the teachers of low achievers meant paying attention to the quality of our entire teaching corps and to public education in general. A teacher licensed for teaching a specific subject at a specific range of grades can legally teach in any public school in the state awarding the license.

There must have been some understanding of the depths of the educational problem facing the entire nation before 1965 because a purpose of ESEA was to "strengthen public education." But those words disappeared in subsequent reauthorizations of ESEA, and eventually, the purposes of ESEA were distorted to mean chiefly "gap closing," a very different goal than strengthening public education for all.

During a brief interlude after World War II, the deteriorating public-school curriculum was being addressed by academic experts working with K–12 teachers, especially in mathematics, science, and English. All sought a much stronger curriculum for all students. But as a participant in the National Defense Education Act (NDEA) institutes of the 1960s observed decades later,

> Our experience in the Curriculum Reform movement shows that the contributions of scholars and scientists are necessary to make good curricula. However, scholars' intellectual authority alone does not suffice for the long term. We need excellent teacher training more than we need anything else. We need to train teachers in subject matter, and to teach them how to teach our lessons while they are still in training. We need to give in-service teachers both solid training in subject matter and the kinds of lessons they want to teach. We need to show them how to teach these lessons, and to give them day-to-day support.[2]

But nothing much was done for decades after 1965 by any state or private foundation to strengthen our teacher corps. And this despite the example of the Flexner report in 1910, which led to two types of quality controls at the state level for medical training: increased admission requirements to medical schools (selective admissions) and tough state licensure tests for graduates of a medical training program. Within several decades, all medical schools in the United States and Canada had closed or been transformed into first-class training schools for medical doctors (in other words, the academic demands of their training were equally high across open medical schools regardless of zip code), with training programs following the recommendations in the Flexner report for a stronger science-based curriculum and well-supervised clinical internships.

Similar mechanisms could have been built into each state's teacher-preparation programs, too. Instead, public officials at the Department of Education who guided implementation of ESEA funds since 1965 concentrated first on remediation for minority students and then on tests for these and other students in the public schools, not on tests, remediation, or academic requirements for their prospective teachers, despite the findings in the Coleman report.

Where did that test of teachers' verbal skills, mentioned in the Coleman report, come from? The report explains that Coleman and his team developed a test of verbal skills to give to large numbers of teachers, black and white, because no test results from a common test that all had taken were available. As the report notes in its introductory section,

> It should be noted that many characteristics of teachers were not measured in this survey; therefore, the results are not at all conclusive regarding the specific characteristics of teachers that are most important. Among those measured in the survey, however, those that bear the highest relationship to pupil achievement are first, the teacher's score on the verbal skills test, and then his educational background, both his own level of education and that of his parents. On both of these measures, the level of teachers of minority students, especially Negroes, is lower.[3]

The Coleman report emphasizes not only what it means by "teacher quality" but also why it means that ("teacher quality seems more important to minority achievement than to that of the majority"[4]). As one can see here, aside from the differences in teachers' verbal skills and educational backgrounds, other differences, if there were any, were of less importance:

> Compared to teachers of the average white student, teachers of the average Negro score lower on a test of verbal competence, and the difference is most pronounced in the Southern States; are neither more nor less likely to have advanced degrees; have slightly more teaching experience and slightly more tenure in their present school; read more professional journals; are neither more nor less likely to have majored in an academic subject; if they are elementary teachers, were less likely to be trained in teachers colleges; more often are products of colleges that offer no graduate training; attended colleges with a much lower percent white in the student body; less often rate their college high in academic quality; less often are members of academic honorary societies, at least in the South; more often participate in teachers' organ-

izations, especially in the South; and more often have attended institutes for the culturally disadvantaged.

Compared to the average white pupil, the average Negro pupil attends a school in which the teachers are neither more nor less likely to have high absenteeism rates; paid more in some regions and less in others, thus the national averages are about the same; more likely to have requested assignment to their particular school and to expect to make a lifelong career of teaching; less likely to wish to remain in their present school if given a chance to change, or to declare they would re-enter teaching if the decision could be made again; less likely to rate students high on academic motivation and ability; less likely to believe that the school has a good reputation with other teachers; less likely (0) to prefer to teach in an academic high school; more likely to spend a substantial amount of time in class preparation; more likely to teach large classes; more likely to spend time counseling students; somewhat more likely to have taught in the school the prior year; and more likely to take a teacher's examination as a condition of employment. [5]

In addition to whatever differences that Coleman and his team found between teachers of mostly white children and teachers of mostly nonwhite children, they also note areas of agreement, including one that is a contentious issue today: "that it is educationally sound to have white teachers for nonwhite pupils and nonwhite faculties for white pupils."[6]

TEACHER QUALITY ACCORDING TO THE COLEMAN REPORT

It is important to grasp what James Coleman and his academic team mean by "teacher quality." Nowhere is there any implication that it refers to "teaching effectiveness" or to the outcomes of a young student's education—as important as they were at the time and since then. The Coleman report is usually clear that teacher quality refers to the teacher's academic skills and background (such as college major or college minor, coursework taken, and the quality of the undergraduate college attended). In contrast, today, it often designates teaching effectiveness *instead of* the teacher's academic background.

However teacher quality is defined today, it usually is the chief, if not the only, education factor related to student achievement, as the Task Group on Teachers and Teacher Education for the National Mathematics Advisory Panel stresses in its final report in 2008.[7] But what exactly "teacher quality" is—what student achievement is actually related to—depends on a researcher's definition of the phrase. Otherwise, research on teacher quality is meaningless. Teacher quality needs to include some measures of a teacher's academic background, *not* students' test scores or whether the teacher holds a teaching license, if policy makers are serious about strengthening it.

Coleman and his colleagues make it reasonably clear that teacher quality refers to the academic knowledge and skills teachers brought to their teaching positions from their own education. Policies to strengthen our teaching corps could have been suggested by the Department of Education in exchange for Title I funds (as it did for beginning reading skills taught to practicing teachers in No Child Left Behind, or NCLB, the 2001 reauthorization of ESEA). However, we know in retrospect that under any circumstances and no matter what the Department of Education expected, it would have been difficult for this country to strengthen teacher-preparation programs academically, given the struggle even today to raise the bar for admission to such a program. Moreover, most academic coursework for prospective teachers is typically located in a college for the arts (or humanities) and sciences, not in an education school.

After success in making the case that teacher quality refers chiefly to pedagogical training, education schools have used low achievement as justification for increasing the number of pedagogically oriented courses a prospective teacher must take, none of which has been shown to improve student achievement. Indeed, the number of education school credits a prospective teacher must earn today in order to complete a teacher-preparation program is much higher than the number required fifty years ago.

When national teacher examinations (NTE) were first proposed and drafted (1930s and 1940s), they emphasized content knowledge. But they were undermined by education school faculty insisting that pedagogy, not content, was what aspiring teachers should be assessed on for licensure and that teaching effectiveness was the chief, if not only, criterion for determining test validity.[8]

Most other teacher licensure tests of content knowledge were also undermined by policies (as in the Race to the Top grant competition in 2010) insisting that teaching effectiveness was what mattered in teacher evaluations, not the teacher's command of the subject(s) he or she was licensed to teach. The two should be related to some extent, of course, but a teacher's academic background can be judged long before the teacher is hired.

What has been almost lost today is the understanding that the validity of a subject area licensure test depends on the relationship of its content to the content of the discipline addressed by the test (i.e., construct validity), not to the teacher's effectiveness in future classrooms using value-added measures. This point lies obscurely at the heart of Dan Goldhaber's comments in his article in the Spring 2016 issue of *Education Next*. His article does not address what teachers should be held accountable for: for what they bring to their teaching of X when hired or for their relationship to student achievement via a statewide test. One can read Goldhaber's two paragraphs here dozens of times, and it becomes no clearer what teacher quality means—

teacher mastery of the subject matter or the kind and number of methods courses teachers have taken:

> The research showing the important variation in teacher quality within schools and its connection not only to test scores but also to other important outcomes ought to strengthen arguments for teacher-oriented policy interventions. But it is precisely the focus on teacher evaluation—and whether it is connected to student test scores—that is at the center of the most hotly contested education policy debates.
>
> Recent revisions to the most prominent federal law dealing with school quality—the Elementary and Secondary Education Act—mark a sharp roll-back of the federal role in teacher evaluation and accountability. It is not clear whether states and localities will consequently focus less attention on teacher quality, but if this is the outcome, policymakers will have failed to internalize the important lesson of both the Coleman Report and subsequent research: the main way that schools affect student outcomes is through the quality of their teachers.[9]

SHOULD PROSPECTIVE ELEMENTARY TEACHERS BE EXPECTED TO PASS AN ELEMENTARY MATH LICENSURE TEST?

The issue (whether teachers need stronger coursework in pedagogy or academic content) has arisen most recently with respect to the validity of an elementary mathematics licensure test for prospective elementary teachers, although it has not been framed that way. The battleground for the argument over this issue is North Carolina. Hundreds of prospective elementary teachers had failed the test since its inception. Ann Doss Helms claims that the problem was likely the test itself.[10] To understand why the test was likely *not* the problem and that the root of the problem was more likely test takers' lack of preparation for the test, we need to know something about this test and its origin.

The test in question was developed in Massachusetts. In 2006, the Bay State's board of education decided that K–8 mathematics knowledge should be assessed for prospective elementary (and special education) teachers on a stand-alone licensure test (a test with an independent cut-off score for passing), not as part of a multisubject test. In December 2006, it approved the development of such a test.

Consisting of forty test items, the test was based on the reasonable expectation that aspiring elementary teachers should be able to demonstrate, without the use of a calculator, a deep understanding of the mathematical concepts that underpin what they would teach their students, also without the use of calculators. Clearly, there was good reason to think that any group of prospective teachers would have already obtained a strong understanding of prealgebra mathematics. After all, they had completed elementary, middle, and high school themselves—years earlier—and had been required to study mathematics at most grade levels.

The elementary mathematics test went into effect in the Bay State in 2009. The test was developed and vetted by the state's own mathematics educators and mathematicians; moreover, only 60 percent of the items needed to be correct for a passing score. A startlingly low percentage of test takers (27 percent) passed on the first test administration, suggesting how such a test was needed. Opposition to the board's vote of approval for an official pass score based on 60 percent correct came only from the state affiliate of the National Education Association. [11] Officials of mathematics organizations in the state approved the test and the cut-off score (at least, they expressed no opposition to them), and one of the two minority members of the board of education (at the time) indicated that academic quality came first, diversity second, in response to concerns expressed by two white board members about how many minority members would pass if 60 percent correct was required.

There is no information available on what happens to test takers who never pass the mathematics portion of the test, no matter how many times they take it. They cannot teach legally in the Bay State's public schools without a license, so there is a strong incentive to prepare for and to pass the test. Nevertheless, the numbers who fail this test, even when they retake it, are very high in Massachusetts. The pass rate has hovered around 50 percent on average over test administrations.

In 2012, on recommendation from North Carolina's Department of Public Instruction, the North Carolina State Board of Education voted to adopt the Massachusetts test. The North Carolina superintendent of public instruction at the time likely helped to set the pass score (cut-off score) for the state. It may or may not be identical to the pass score in the Bay State. The testing company provided a shorter practice test similar to the one-hundred-item practice test it provided in the Bay State to suggest how difficult the actual test may be, although not all training programs in North Carolina necessarily require prospective elementary teachers to use it. Nor do they necessarily require aspiring elementary teachers to take the recommended elementary mathematics coursework described in the *Guidelines for the Mathematical Preparation of Elementary Teachers* developed in the Bay State to help teacher-preparation programs provide the right coursework to prepare their students for the test. [12]

The mathematicians, mathematics educators, and others who developed the Massachusetts test developed these 2007 guidelines for the elementary mathematics courses these aspiring teachers should have taken before taking the licensure test in elementary mathematics. The guidelines also indicate what topics should be taught in mathematics coursework for prospective elementary teachers, preferably by people with advanced degrees in mathematics.

How the conflict about requiring this elementary mathematics licensure test in North Carolina will play out remains to be seen. But the animus against licensure tests for teachers is growing, as a 2017 article about Florida suggests.[13] The basic questions about licensure tests for teachers have yet to be discussed publicly. Are such tests to have relatively low cut-off scores to protect the putative right of any adult who wishes to be a teacher, or are they to have high enough cut-off scores to protect students from academically incompetent teachers?

Or are states to have weak or no teacher licensure tests at all and implicitly facilitate nepotism or quotas of some kind in school hiring practices? The authors of the Coleman report imply that schools need to protect minority students from academically inadequate teachers.

WHY CONGRESS DIDN'T STRENGTHEN
TEACHER-PREPARATION PROGRAMS

Why does legislation in reauthorizations of ESEA and in many grant programs talk about "failing" or "low-performing" schools or focus on "poverty" as the source of low achievement and do little, if anything, to strengthen academically their teachers? Among the many possible reasons, it has not been easy for the Department of Education to claim that some teachers know more or less than other teachers. Using student test scores as the measure, it has been easier to claim that teachers are not teaching some students as well as they should on the grounds that teachers are bigoted and hold very low expectations for some students than to claim that their teachers don't know the subjects they teach well enough.

It has certainly been unclear (then and now) how general academic demands on prospective teachers can be strengthened at a time when political leaders and education schools claim they need more teachers, not fewer. The higher the bar, the fewer prospective teachers will pass it. But how can Congress legitimately raise the bar without unacceptable implications? Only the families of minority or immigrant children can demand a higher bar.

The first clear link between federal aid and a requirement for academically strong teachers came with the No Child Left Behind Act in 2001–2002. It sought to get school districts to require the use of only highly qualified teachers (HQT). This meant that schools would have to take into account both what a teacher had majored in as an undergraduate and a score on a subject-matter licensure test.[14] However, states were allowed to define HQT as they saw fit and to require an approved professional-development program as the way to strengthen their current teachers. In other words, states could backload but were not required to frontload.

In fact, schools did define HQT in many ways in order to grandfather in older, experienced teachers who did not have a strong undergraduate major in the subject they taught. But there is no evidence that these provisions in NCLB strengthened subject-matter teachers. Nor is there evidence that professional development in general increases student achievement.[15]

SUMMARY

Although the Coleman report found that the "teachers of white children differed from the teachers of Negro children in average verbal skills," Congress did almost nothing in the following decades to strengthen academically teachers of African American students or other students in our public schools. The language on "highly qualified teachers" in No Child Left Behind (the reauthorization of ESEA in 2001) was the first time that public policy paid attention to teachers' academic backgrounds. And the chief way that in-service teachers could be upgraded academically was by means of professional development (after the fact), not before they began teaching. The burden for upgrading teacher quality was on professional development.

However, to this day, it is almost impossible to find well-designed studies showing professional development useful in developing teachers' general knowledge of the subject they teach. There is no evidence showing that teacher professional development can substitute for real coursework in the subject. It is not surprising that practicing teachers cannot develop a greater understanding of the subject they teach through short professional-development workshops—long after they have completed undergraduate coursework—either at the end of a tiring workday or at a weekend retreat.

One can legitimately wonder if professional development should be required at all for teachers. Professional development may be effective in demonstrating a new strategy in reading or providing information on a new topic in science or history, but that may be about all. Indeed, no other country spends what we spend on professional development—probably because they know it does not make sense to try to teach practicing teachers what they should have learned in regular coursework as undergraduates or in master's programs before becoming teachers.

KEY IDEAS TO REMEMBER

1. In the Coleman report, teachers of "white" children differed from the teachers of African American children in average verbal skills.

2. According to the Coleman report, teachers are "one of the few school characteristics that significantly affects student performance."

3. Congress did relatively nothing after the 1958 NDEA institutes to strengthen American teachers academically until it required in 2001 a "highly qualified" teacher in the No Child Left Behind Act.

4. Teacher quality at first meant teachers' academic background, not changes in student scores on tests that teachers didn't construct or vet.

5. The first national teacher examinations (NTE) emphasized content knowledge and were undermined by education schools insisting that pedagogy, not content, was what all aspiring teachers should be assessed for licensure. Educators also claimed that teaching effectiveness determined test validity.

6. Reviews of research on teacher professional development provide little support for the idea that it can substitute for real coursework in the subject. It does not increase student achievement. It is chiefly remedial in nature and, in many teachers' eyes, mostly a waste of time and money.

NOTES

1. James S. Coleman, Ernest Q. Campbell, Carol J. Hobson, James McPartland, Alexander M. Mood, Frederic D. Weinfeld, and Robert L. York, *Equality of Educational Opportunity* (Washington, DC: US Government Printing Office, 1966), 335, https://files.eric.ed.gov/fulltext/ED012275.pdf.

2. Mary Campbell Gallagher, "Chapter 12: Lessons from the Sputnik-Era Curriculum Reform Movement: The Institutions We Need for Educational Reform," in *What's at Stake in the K–12 Standards Wars: A Primer for Educational Policy Makers*, edited by Sandra Stotsky (New York: Peter Lang, 2000), 312.

3. Coleman et al., *Equality of Educational Opportunity*, 22.

4. Coleman et al., *Equality of Educational Opportunity*, 22.

5. Coleman et al., *Equality of Educational Opportunity*, 147, 166.

6. Coleman et al., *Equality of Educational Opportunity*, 183.

7. Deborah Loewenberg Ball, James Simons, Hung-Hsi Wu, Raymond Simon, Grover J. "Russ" Whitehurst, and Jim Yun, "Chapter 5: Report of the Task Group on Teachers and Teacher Education," in *Foundations for Success: The Final Report of the National Mathematics Advisory Panel* (Washington, DC: US Department of Education, 2008), 5–7, https://www2.ed.gov/about/bdscomm/list/mathpanel/report/teachers.pdf.

8. See chapter 4 in Sandra Stotsky, *An Empty Curriculum: The Need to Reform Teacher Licensing Regulations and Tests* (Lanham, MD: Rowman & Littlefield, 2015).

9. Dan Goldhaber, "In Schools, Teacher Quality Matters Most—Today's Research Reinforces Coleman's Findings," *EducationNext* 16, no. 2 (Spring 2016), http://educationnext.org/in-schools-teacher-quality-matters-most-coleman.

10. Ann Doss Helms, "Hundreds of NC Teachers Are Flunking Math Exam. It May Not Be Their Fault," *Charlotte Observer*, August 2, 2018, https://www.charlotteobserver.com/news/local/education/article215848065.html.

11. Minutes of the regular meeting of the Massachusetts Board of Elementary and Secondary Education, May 19, 2009, https://studylib.net/doc/15155376/0519reg.

12. Tom Fortmann, *Guidelines for the Mathematical Preparation of Elementary Teachers* (Malden: Massachusetts Department of Education, July 2007), http://www.doe.mass.edu/mtel/mathguidance.pdf.

13. Katie Lagrone and Matthew Apthorp, "More Teachers Are Failing State-Mandated FTCE, Florida Teacher Certification Exam," *WFTS Tampa Bay*, February 3, 2017, https://www.abcactionnews.com/longform/teachers-failing-state-certification-test-at-alarming-rates.

14. Wikipedia Contributors, "Highly Qualified Teachers," *Wikipedia*, updated January 13, 2019, https://en.wikipedia.org/wiki/Highly_qualified_teachers. Title II in the 2001 reauthorization of ESEA had come from the old Eisenhower grants of 1985 (the congressional response to *A Nation at Risk* released in 1983).

15. See, for example, Ball et al., "Chapter 5"; Russell Gersten, Mary Jo Taylor, Tran D. Keys, Eric Rolfhus, and Rebecca Newman-Gonchar, *Summary of Research on the Effectiveness of Math Professional Development Approaches* (Washington DC: National Center for Evaluation and Regional Assistance, Institute of Educational Sciences, 2014), https://ies.ed.gov/ncee/edlabs/regions/southeast/pdf/REL_2014010.pdf.

Chapter Four

Nonschool Factors Influencing Low Achievement

This chapter examines the nonschool factors mentioned in the 1966 Coleman report and elsewhere. They need to be looked at because, together, they helped to define "family background" in the report. Recall that the factors associated with "family background" carried more weight than school-related factors in explaining or determining academic achievement, according to the Coleman team's statistical analyses.

NONSCHOOL FACTORS EXAMINED IN THE COLEMAN REPORT

What exactly did that part of the equation consist of? The tables in the report's appendixes, especially from the section on "reliability of question-naire responses" to the end of this massive report (from about p. 570 on) indicate the many nonschool factors for which information was obtained—from students, their teachers, and their principals. Despite the practical problems in obtaining accurate information from children, the report's authors believe that the information they got from children was generally honest. [1]

Among the many topics for which Coleman's team got information were

1. Parents' education
2. Structure of home (e.g., two-parent family)
3. If the mother worked outside the home
4. Books and other items in the home, what parents read
5. Parents' interests and educational desires for children
6. Stability of home (how much moving around)

7. Number of children in the home
8. Number of rooms in the home
9. Stability of parents (divorce, remarriage, partners)
10. Peers
11. Neighborhood
12. Foreign languages spoken in the home

THE 1965 MOYNIHAN REPORT

It is unknown if any private or public agencies succeeded in strengthening "family background" after the Coleman report was issued in 1966. Both education researchers and civil rights organizations have never mentioned any efforts to do so. This is surprising, given that an earth-shaking report was released in 1965, anticipating the central finding of the Coleman report and giving it more weight.

The Negro Family: The Case for National Action was written by Daniel Patrick Moynihan, a sociologist who at the time was a political appointee at the US Department of Labor, hired to help develop policy for the Johnson administration in its War on Poverty.[2] He served as assistant secretary of labor for President Johnson.

According to Wikipedia, his report (also known as the Moynihan report) focuses on the "deep roots of black poverty in the United States and controversially [concludes] that the high rate of families headed by single mothers would greatly hinder progress of blacks toward economic and political equality."[3] The Moynihan report argues that the black family, "battered and harassed by discrimination, . . . is the fundamental source of the weakness of the Negro community. . . . In fact, the percentage of black children born to unmarried mothers . . . tripled between the early 1960s and 2009, remaining far higher than the percentage of white children born to unmarried mothers."[4]

More specifically, Moynihan attributes the large disparities between the numbers of black and white children born into and raised in single-parent households and the black and white marriage rates as the key factors impeding black economic progress and social equality: "Black poverty and unemployment rates are far higher than those of whites, black children are far more likely to be born into and raised in single-parent households than white children, and black teens and adults are far more likely to be imprisoned." The report concludes that the structure of family life in the black community constituted a "tangle of pathology . . . capable of perpetuating itself without assistance from the white world."

The phrase about "pathology" and the claim that the weak structure of black family life retarded black movement toward equality aroused immense hostility from all positions on the political spectrum. Among Moynihan's many critics was William Ryan, a psychology professor at Boston College who coined the phrase "blaming the victim" in his 1971 book *Blaming the Victim*, a critique of the Moynihan report. He asserts that the report is an attempt to divert responsibility for poverty from the larger society to the behavioral patterns and the culture of the poor themselves. A host of Moynihan's critics seemingly accused him of blaming the black family for the failure of Reconstruction itself. Much, if not most, of the critics' energy ended up in rages against whites; little energy went into coming up with solutions.

It would not be remiss to view the Moynihan report as the immediate political context for the first authorization of the Elementary and Secondary Education Act (ESEA), passed just a month after its release. At this point in time (i.e., 2019), it is possible to believe that well-intentioned policy makers and legislators in 1965 expected the schools to remedy and undo the "tangle of pathology" and do it without damaging their own institutional mission. These policy makers (including Moynihan himself) may have had little understanding of what was happening in K–12 and education schools for about a decade. Did they know much about the criticisms of American education since the end of World War II; the reasons for the National Defense Education Act (NDEA) institutes, in mathematics and science especially; or the controversy over the causes of the huge drop in SAT verbal and mathematics scores in 1963?

ESEA allocated a huge amount of federal money for the education of "disadvantaged" children in low-income communities (Title I), to be spent and monitored chiefly by the Department of Education and educators in the schools, but instead, it could have allocated most of the money to the Department of Labor or to Public Health Institutes for projects or policies that might directly influence black employment and family structure. Perhaps Congress (and the president and his advisors) felt that these other areas had been taken care of by the federal government in the Civil Rights Act of 1964. It would have been worth the effort trying to think of a more appropriate federal agency to address family structure (and not expect the Office of Education to manage all the funds). But there are no "Madison's Notes" on such discussions, if they took place.

The question to think about is why the thrust of the Moynihan report was followed by the 1965 authorization of ESEA. The purpose of the whole act was "to strengthen and improve educational quality and educational opportunities in the Nation's elementary and secondary schools."[5] The purpose of Title I was "Financial Assistance to Local Educational Agencies for the Education of Children of Low-Income Families and Extension of Public Law 874, Eighty-First Congress." Neither has anything to do with employment and black family structure, but ESEA did reflect a lot of political squabbling about the nature and reach of a federal role in education, as described by

Patrick McGuinn and Frederick Hess in the paper "Freedom from Ignorance? The Great Society and the Evolution of the Elementary and Secondary Education Act of 1965."[6]

As McGuinn and Hess note, "One of the fundamental premises behind the idea of compensatory education, and of ESEA more generally, was that state and local education authorities had failed to ensure equal educational opportunities for their students and that they could not be trusted to do so in the future without federal intervention." They further note, "While the design and priorities of some federal programs were questioned, the central idea that the federal government had an obligation to expand the opportunities of the disadvantaged through new programs and resources was widely accepted during the 1970s by politicians and the public alike." There was no discussion about what to do next if the "new programs and resources" accomplished little—or had negative results. In other words, no plan B.

In one sense, ESEA reflected skepticism about what state and local education agencies could or would do on their own without prodding from the federal government. In a contrasting interpretation, ESEA reflected unearned and unjustified confidence in what they could do. The freedom that local and state educators were given in order to develop better educational programs for minority children still raises the question, Why was there so much faith in state and local education agencies? Educators had not chalked up a record of effectiveness in addressing low achievement even before the rapid expansion of public high schools in the early decades of the twentieth century. They had tried, though.

WHY REMEDIAL READING WAS THE FIRST APPROACH TO ADDRESS LOW ACHIEVEMENT

At the turn of the twentieth century, urban educators had had to address the needs of many adolescents (often immigrants or children of immigrants) who may have reluctantly attended high school because of federal child labor laws and state-level compulsory attendance laws. To keep the children of English-language or middle-income families in the public schools (and school budgets supported by the local community) and to entice students to attend grade 9 in a junior high school and continue on to high school, educators introduced optional curriculum "tracks," differing ability levels for some high school courses, and ability grouping in newly formed junior high schools.

Educators throughout the country had done their best to teach and keep students in public schools until they left to help their families on a farm or in a family business or to apprentice with a tradesman (at around age fourteen). The chief strategy that educators thought could directly address widespread low achievement in children and adolescents in school was a remedial class in reading. This possibility likely resulted from the fact that reading research had begun in the early twentieth century, and reading tutorials and remedial programs had begun to develop soon afterward. Because reading was the basic subject in the school curriculum, remedial reading classes made sense.

Policy makers in the 1960s may not have realized, despite the Moynihan report, that only the stability of the black family could make the related components of black poverty, such as illiteracy and unemployment, addressable. James Patterson notes that Moynihan bolded the following statement in the closing section of his report: "The policy of the United States [should be] to bring the Negro American to full and equal sharing in the responsibilities and rewards of citizenship. To this end, the programs of the Federal government bearing on this objective shall be designed to have the effect, directly or indirectly, of enhancing the stability and resources of the Negro American family."[7] These were brave words, but the thrust of the programs of the federal government "bearing on this objective" has been educational in nature. If civil rights organizations thought this was too narrow a direction to go in, they didn't let policy makers know, and they still don't.

Several years after President Johnson's War on Poverty began, Moynihan's advice on what to do about racial tensions is captured by his phrase "benign neglect," which appeared in a famous memo to President Richard Nixon in 1970.[8] The phrase aroused even more anger than his 1965 report had among those who wanted immediate solutions to the issues creating racial tensions in this country. Columnist George Will explains Moynihan's phrase: "His point in saying that the subject of race could benefit from a period of 'benign neglect' was to encourage 'some equivalence between what government can do about certain problems and how much attention it draws to them.'"[9] Will's explanation didn't help. The phrase was interpreted again by Moynihan's critics as a way to blame the victim.

Because both "benign neglect" and experimental research-based policies on non-school-related factors were unacceptable to those interested in improving the living conditions and the education of low-achieving black children, Congress and state organizations had little choice but to continue funding what they thought were promising educational policies or programs as a demonstration of their basic concern. Little else happened for decades to strengthen the education of black children until the reauthorization of ESEA in 2001 (No Child Left Behind, or NCLB) under President Bush required schools to report test scores for racial and other demographic groups in order to show whether they achieved adequate yearly progress (AYP). The concept of test-based accountability was considered a breakthrough; schools were held "accountable" for all subgroups' progress, not just for scores for the school as a whole. Test-based accountability for all subgroups was also built into Race to the Top (a competitive grant program in Arne Duncan's Department of Education) and the reauthorization of ESEA in 2015 (Every Student Succeeds Act, or ESSA) under President Obama. Since the waning of the NDEA institutes, the need to strengthen the curriculum for all students was forgotten, if not deliberately rejected as a goal of public education.

Because African Americans as a demographic group appear at the bottom of every academic index the Department of Education can come up with, it may seem that either bigotry has been deepening at a faster pace than congressional appropriations for ESEA have been increasing or the wrong institutions were given the responsibility for increasing black achievement. The "gaps" between higher and lower performers have not closed, despite the ever-increasing amount of money going to low-performing schools.[10] But no specific constructive policies have been forthcoming from any relevant organization.

In 2013, the Urban Institute issued "The Moynihan Report Revisited," which concludes,

> Debates about the status and progress of black families in the United States started before the Moynihan Report and have clearly raged since. The report focused on how black family structure contributed to a host of factors that all impeded progress toward social equity. In the decades since its release, many of the social trends that concerned Moynihan have worsened for blacks and non-blacks alike. Today it is clear that no one factor by itself holds the key to economic and social progress.[11]

The Urban Institute offers no specific recommendations at the end of its report, and its website in 2018 has no suggestions to address family stability or education.[12]

The 2018 education positions of the National Association for the Advancement of Colored People (NAACP) also offer little guidance to education policy makers.[13] Like the US Chamber of Commerce Foundation, with which it collaborates, and unlike the Urban Institute, it doesn't mention the Moynihan report or black family structure.[14] According to the NAACP, someone or something is to ensure "access to great teaching, equitable resources, and a challenging curriculum."

To achieve these goals, the Education Committee of the national board, in concert with education chairs and leaders from across the association, settled on a four-prong strategy to improve educational achievement for disadvantaged students, even if in turnaround schools:

1. Increasing resource equity: target funds to neediest kids
2. Ensuring college and career readiness: a path to success after graduation for all students
3. Improving teaching: growing our own great teachers now in underserved communities
4. Improving discipline: eliminate zero tolerance; keep kids in school

No acknowledgment here that nothing has worked or worked well for more than fifty years. Instead, it supports a set of standards today that widens the "gaps," and it wants more black teachers to be responsible for low achievement in low-performing schools. The US Chamber of Commerce Foundation's 2015 report acknowledges, "Education equity is a complex problem, and no one-size-fits-all solution exists."[15] But it offers no clue about where to start.

The belief that there is no one place to begin in order to solve a complex problem permeates most discussions today, as does the blame game. While lip service to family stability (and black unemployment) can be found, no policies that stand a reasonable chance of public acceptance have been proposed.

We find what may be viewed as a final word on the subject in the 2015 issue of *EducationNext* commemorating the Moynihan report. Sara McLanahan, professor of sociology and public affairs at Princeton University, and Christopher Jencks, professor of social policy at the Harvard Kennedy School, conclude,

> Nonetheless, postponing fertility will not solve the problem of non-marital childbearing unless the economic prospects of the young men who father the children also improve. Women are not likely to marry men whom they view as poor providers, regardless of their own earning capacity. Thus, in addition to encouraging young women to delay motherhood, we also need to improve the economic prospects of their prospective husbands, especially those with no more than a high school diploma. This will not be easy. But it would improve the lives of the men in question, perhaps reduce their level of antisocial behavior, and improve the lives of their children, through all the benefits that flow from a stable home.[16]

In the meantime, public education has continued to deteriorate for all students, including the "disadvantaged." No policies pointing to remedies, no partial solutions, and no commonsense K–12 guidelines from the Department of Education emerged from a 2005 article in *City Journal* on the topic.[17]

One looks in vain at blogger RiShawn Biddle's comments after a rebroadcast of a *Dropout Nation* podcast from 2012 or at Ta-Nehisi Coates's 2015 article in the *Atlantic* for hints on policies that would "make teachers equally effective for all students, regardless of race," as Thomas Dee states in his 2004 essay in *EducationNext*.[18] Somehow schoolteachers and administrators today are supposed to untangle the pathologies growing from the history of bigotry and slavery hundreds of years ago.

Biddle calls on reformers to "remember the need to build brighter futures for all kids" in a rebroadcast of his 2012 podcast.[19] But he does not offer any education policies he would put into place to advance "systemic reform." Another writer who identifies herself as black says black students don't need black teachers. What she proposes, instead, are "good black teachers."[20] Ta-

Nehisi Coates writes very well but in the final analysis offers readers only his anger.[21] He mentions "reparations," but even if black and white teachers teach that Congress should pass a policy of reparations, black students won't become literate and numerate with its passage.

SUMMARY

Almost everyone acknowledges that stable families are better for all children than unstable families. But no untried recommendations to improve the education of black children have been offered. Charter schools have an unelected form of governance, making them, in the final analysis, unaccountable and therefore unacceptable to taxpayers at all levels of government. The basic error in policy making was expecting the schools (administrators and teachers) to solve the "tangle of pathology," as Moynihan describes the situation in his 1965 report.

Because black children begin kindergarten already behind their peers, their schools and teachers are clearly not the cause of their low achievement. Why are teachers (black, white, Asian, or Hispanic), who might be in charge of black students for no more than twenty-five hours a week, to be held accountable for their students' scores on tests they didn't create or review? Even if they had created the tests or reviewed those mandated by the state, why are teachers, instead of the policy makers, held accountable for the results?

KEY IDEAS TO REMEMBER

1. Among the many factors in "family background" that the Coleman team gathered information on was parents' education, structure of the home, and stability of the parents.
2. Both the 1965 Moynihan report and the 1966 Coleman report saw the single-parent home as a weakness of the black family.
3. The Moynihan report can be considered the immediate political context for the first authorization of ESEA, passed in April 1965.
4. The first authorization of ESEA said nothing about black employment and black family structure, but one of its purposes was strengthening the school curriculum for all students.
5. To date, no civil rights or African American organizations have recommended specific policies to address the central findings of the Moynihan or Coleman reports.

NOTES

1. James S. Coleman, Ernest Q. Campbell, Carol J. Hobson, James McPartland, Alexander M. Mood, Frederic D. Weinfeld, and Robert L. York, *Equality of Educational Opportunity* (Washington, DC: US Government Printing Office, 1966), 569, https://files.eric.ed.gov/fulltext/ED012275.pdf. The authors of the Coleman report note, "It may be concluded, bearing in mind the limitations of this study that were described above, that pupils responded to the questionnaire used for this survey with reasonable accuracy to factual items about themselves, their schooling, and their homes and families."

2. *The Negro Family: The Case for National Action* (Office of Policy Planning and Research, US Department of Labor, March 1965), https://www.dol.gov/general/aboutdol/history/webid-moynihan. The report consists of forty-eight pages of text, sixty-one footnotes, and a twenty-four-page appendix of charts and tables.

3. "*The Negro Family: The Case for National Action*," Wikipedia, updated February 13, 2019, https://en.wikipedia.org/wiki/The_Negro_Family:_The_Case_For_National_Action.

4. Gregory Acs, Kenneth Braswell, Elaine Sorensen, and Margery Austin Turner, *The Moynihan Report Revisited* (Washington, DC: Urban Institute, June 2013), https://www.urban.org/research/publication/moynihan-report-revisited/view/full_report.

5. Elementary and Secondary Education Act of 1965, H.R. 2362, 89th Cong. (1965).

6. The paper is published as chapter 11 in Sidney M. Milkis and Jerome M. Mileur, eds., *The Great Society and the High Tide of Liberalism* (Amherst: University of Massachusetts Press, 2005).

7. James T. Patterson, "Moynihan and the Single-Parent Family," *EducationNext* 15, no. 2 (Spring 2015), https://www.educationnext.org/moynihan-and-the-single-parent-family/.

8. "Benign Neglect," Encyclopedia.com, 2008, https://www.encyclopedia.com/history/united-states-and-canada/us-history/benign-neglect.

9. George F. Will, "The Wisdom of Pat Moynihan," *Washington Post*, October 3, 2010, http://www.washingtonpost.com/wp-dyn/content/article/2010/10/01/AR2010100105262.html.

10. Sandra D. Sparks, "Nation's Report Card: Achievement Flattens as Gaps Widen between High and Low Performers," *Education Week*, April 10, 2018, http://blogs.edweek.org/edweek/inside-school-research/2018/04/nations_report_card_2018_us_achievement.html.

11. Acs et al., *Moynihan Report Revisited*.

12. "From Safety Net to Solid Ground," Urban Institute, accessed February 15, 2019, https://www.urban.org/features/safety-net-solid-ground.

13. "Education," NAACP, 2019, https://www.naacp.org/issues/education/.

14. "The Path Forward: Improving Opportunities for African-American Students," US Chamber of Commerce Foundation, December 10, 2015, https://www.uschamberfoundation.org/reports/path-forward-improving-opportunities-african-american-students.

15. US Chamber of Commerce Foundation, *The Path Forward: Improving Opportunities for African-American Students* (Washington, DC: US Chamber of Commerce Foundation, 2015), 34, https://www.uschamberfoundation.org/sites/default/files/The_Path_Forward_Report_Final.pdf.

16. Sara McLanahan and Christopher Jencks, "Was Moynihan Right?" *EducationNext* 15, no. 5 (Spring 2015), https://www.educationnext.org/was-moynihan-right.

17. Kay S. Hymowitz, "The Black Family: 40 Years of Lies," *City Journal* (Summer 2005), https://www.city-journal.org/html/black-family-40-years-lies-12872.html.

18. Thomas S. Dee, "The Race Connection," *EducationNext* 4, no. 2 (Spring 2004), https://www.educationnext.org/the-race-connection.

19. RiShawn Biddle, "Best of Dropout Nation: The Call to Revolutionize American Public Education," January 3, 2018, https://www.stitcher.com/podcast/dropout-nation-podcast/the-dropout-nation-podcast.

20. Denene Millner, "Black Parents Want Good Teachers, Not Necessarily Black Ones," *My Brown Baby* (blog), June 13, 2012, http://mybrownbaby.com/2012/06/black-parents-want-good-teachers-not-necessarily-black-ones/.

21. Ta-Nehisi Coates, "The Black Family in the Age of Mass Incarceration," *Atlantic*, October 2015, https://www.theatlantic.com/magazine/archive/2015/10/the-black-family-in-the-age-of-mass-incarceration/403246.

Chapter Five

What Noneducation Researchers Have Explored Since 1966

This country has not had much success transforming low achievers into college-ready or career-ready higher achievers using the educational strategies, interventions, and programs recommended or mandated by federal and state educational agencies and boards. Thus, it is not surprising that noneducation researchers have tried to explore noneducation factors that might be related to low achievement. As chapter 2 indicates, the authors of both the 1965 Moynihan report and the 1966 Coleman report (mainly sociologists) conclude from the information they gathered that family-related influences are more important than school- or teacher-related influences for academic achievement. Other areas of research by noneducation researchers can also help us to understand low achievement.

SCIENTIFIC RESEARCH ON TECHNOLOGIES USED IN AND OUT OF SCHOOL

In an attempt to help low achievers or children of low-income families to become familiar with technologies that might help them with future career choices, the US Department of Education approved state plans for ESSA mandating that state standardized tests be taken online. All students from grade 3 on were required to take state tests on a computer and therefore had to learn keyboarding skills at a very young age. This peculiar federal mandate was accompanied by a rise in the use of other technologies in regular classrooms and for homework for both teachers and students.

Researchers are now looking at the effects of different kinds of technologies used in classrooms and at home regarding privacy.[1] Some of these researchers are trying to see if there are negative effects from the constant use of different kinds of technologies for teaching, learning, and social communications.[2] Parents and local school boards should welcome scientists' interest in the benefits and disadvantages of the new technologies for student and teacher health. A recent study by the Organization for Economic Cooperation and Development found that countries where fifteen-year-olds use computers in the classroom the most scored the worst on international reading and math tests.

Study of the effects of these technologies is costly, and the extensive use of technology in the classroom has not appeared to pay off for school districts that have made heavy investments in them (and in personnel to maintain them).[3] Nor has the use of computer-based testing yielded more useful information to teachers than the much cheaper paper-and-pencil tests used before.

A 2018 study by the Swiss Tropical and Public Health Institute looked at the effects of excessive mobile phone use on adolescents, something parents and teachers are increasingly concerned about. The study focused on how mobile phone radiation may affect memory development in adolescents and concludes, "Radiofrequency electromagnetic fields may have adverse effects on the development of memory performance of specific brain regions exposed during mobile phone use. These are the findings of a study involving nearly 700 adolescents in Switzerland."[4] These scientists found adverse effects on the development of "figural" memory in the right hemisphere of the brains of adolescents who held a cell phone on their right side when using it for more than a year. One study, however, does not lead to sweeping recommendations.

Some technology is increasingly used for educational purposes, such as for online courses. A 2009 Department of Education review of studies on the effectiveness of online learning found varying benefits for learners. However, many of the studies summarized in this report were not large enough or well designed to permit more definite takeaways. Its authors conclude, "Larger-scale studies are needed to show the correlations between program models, instructional models, technologies, conditions and practices for effective online learning."[5] This suggests that online course learning does not have a large body of evidence to justify a major reliance on it.

Widespread use of new technologies for K–12 students may pose totally new threats to students' health and privacy. The Federal Bureau of Investigation (FBI) issued a public-service announcement on September 13, 2018, urging schools to implement measures that will guard against "cyber threat concerns" and promote greater "cybersecurity," but there is no record of how many local school boards paid any attention to this warning.[6]

MEDICAL AND PUBLIC HEALTH RESEARCH
ON ADOLESCENT SLEEP NEEDS

Research on sleep has boomed in recent decades, in large part because almost half the country's high schools (43 percent, according to one survey) start before 8:00 a.m. Years ago, when *consolidation* and *regionalization* were buzzwords, many sleepy adolescents arrived at school after a long bus ride. Teachers soon noticed late students in early-morning classes, and these numbers have increased. There are many reasons, sometimes combined, for sleep-deprived adolescents: catching an early-morning school bus; excessive use of computers and social media before, during, and after school hours; access to a family car in the evening; too much homework; video games; underage drinking; after-school volunteer work for community-service or college-application requirements; and after-school employment. There are too many contributing factors to have well-controlled studies on the amount and quality of sleep that adolescents get each night.

Because of the many studies suggesting various issues related to lack of sleep for adolescents, doctors and public health workers are thinking about what can be changed most easily.[7] Professionals who have studied sleep-deprived adolescents agree that many factors that significantly affect sleep in teenagers are modifiable. We can alter electronic media use, caffeine consumption, and early school start times, for example. However, there are raging controversies about whether a state legislature or state board of education or a local school board should determine school start times.

The American Academy of Pediatrics urges discussions and systemic evaluations of the "community-wide impact of these changes (e.g., on academic performance, school budget, traffic patterns, teacher retention)."[8] It cautions, "It should also be emphasized that delaying school start times alone is less likely to have a significant effect without concomitant attention to other contributing and potentially remediable factors, such as excessive demands on students' time because of homework, extracurricular activities, after-school employment, social networking, and electronic media use."[9] In other words, a comprehensive approach is needed to effectively address the links between sleep deprivation in adolescents and academic achievement.

To underscore the need for a comprehensive approach to the causes of sleep-deprived adolescents, Leonard Sax, a pediatrician with a doctoral degree in psychology, made several recommendations based on a longitudinal study of the possible relationship between social media use and ADHD.[10] It is probably easier for local school boards to change their votes as medical evidence accumulates than for a state legislature to change state laws it may have hastily enacted.

LEGAL SCHOLARSHIP ON SCHOOL DISCIPLINE

Research and legal scholarship on a school's right to discipline students is fairly recent but very controversial. How a school disciplines its students may affect learning, as claimed in a New York University 2003 press release for sociologist Richard Arum's groundbreaking book:

> Before 1965, there were only a handful of legal challenges in which schools were taken to court over their disciplinary procedures. Since then, there have been more than 1,500 cases in which a school's right to discipline students was contested and considered in U.S. appellate courts. This dramatic turnaround has made school discipline more difficult than ever before and undermined the quality of public education [according to Professor Arum].[11]

Unfortunately, judging from education conferences and professional education journals, Arum's book *Judging School Discipline: The Crisis of Moral Authority* didn't lead to the kind of discussions by school administrators and teachers it warranted. As Arum puts it, litigation contesting a school's right to discipline its students has prevented schools from providing equal educational opportunities for all rather than protecting students' civil liberties.

The issue at the heart of the problem is the possible reasons for the difference in disciplinary rates between black and white students. In an analysis of the Department of Education's proposed use of disparate-impact theory in examining school discipline across the country, the Civil Rights Practice Group offers three ways to interpret differences in disciplinary rates among racially classified groups of students:

> If disparities exist among racial and ethnic groups in school discipline, there are three possible explanations: (1) teachers and school officials are discriminating on the basis of race or national origin; (2) students of different races and national origins misbehave in school at different rates; or (3) a combination of the two. Secretary Duncan and Attorney General Holder seem to believe the first explanation. The underlying premise is that white students, for example, will commit infractions at the same rate as black students.[12]

In effect, this suggests that black students are disciplined more than other groups because white students (and possibly Asian Americans) aren't disciplined enough and need more discipline.

The Civil Rights Practice Group goes on to argue that there are disparities across racial groups in many areas, such as crime rates, "not because of discrimination by police, prosecutors, or courts, but because blacks commit crimes at a higher rate than whites." It further notes that "disparate-impact theory creates an incentive to achieve racially proportionate outcomes," so, in the case of public schools, they can "avoid the loss of federal funds." It worries that the Department of Education's "use of disparate-impact theory may lead to a reduction in good order and discipline in many schools if school boards and principals believe they must weaken their policies to achieve a racial balance."[13]

Debates about the reasons for different racial and ethnic rates of school discipline and what to do about it continue.[14] When schools have proportional rates of disciple across student subgroups, studies do not explain whether academic achievement is enhanced for some or all student groups. Similarly, studies on large disparities in disciplinary rates do not explain whether those differences can be attributed to bigotry on the part of teachers and school administrators. More research is necessary to determine if teachers and schools don't report discipline (possibly to equalize rates across racial groups) or if biases have reduced learning opportunities for black students through overreporting their violations or if both are happening.

SOCIAL SCIENCE RESEARCH ON POVERTY

The possible links between poverty and academic achievement have to be isolated to be understood. Historian Richard Rothstein comments in an *Economic Policy* blog that "lower-class status" is more useful than "poverty" because the concept includes the many related factors that "poverty" usually reflects:

> If we want to raise the achievement of disadvantaged children substantially in our own country, we will have to improve the collection of interacting and mutually reinforcing characteristics of lower social class status. Addressing any one of them alone—whether it be income, or teen childbearing, or some other—will be a good thing to do but won't get us very far on the path we hope to take.[15]

In a June 2015 report issued by the Economic Policy Institute, coauthors Leila Morsy and Richard Rothstein provide five significant features of "lower-class status":

> Of the many social class characteristics known to depress [academic] outcomes, this report deals with five: challenged home intellectual environments, single parenthood, irregular parental work schedules, inadequate health care access, and exposure to environmental lead. These factors were chosen because recent research has offered important new insights regarding each. But these are not the only important characteristics depressing outcomes, nor is there a research basis for determining with any certainty whether they are necessarily the most important.[16]

Unlike many education researchers and educators, Morsy and Rothstein offer a range of policies that might improve both academic and nonacademic outcomes for "disadvantaged" children. Also unlike many educators, these refreshingly honest authors acknowledge that their recommended policies are not evidence-based but are simply "plausible" because, as they indicate, a strong research base does not exist for them.

Among their recommendations are (1) an expansion of Head Start, (2) a national full-employment policy providing jobs "with compensation levels adequate to support families," and (3) work schedules that facilitate a stable home life for children. As their range of recommended policies implies, Morsy and Rothstein understand that schools alone cannot close "achievement gaps." Unfortunately, neither Congress nor the Department of Education has conveyed to state and local school boards other policies and agencies that might supplement their plans for ESSA. ESSA—and state education agencies—simply expects schools and teachers alone to close achievement gaps.

SOCIAL SCIENCE RESEARCH ON FAMILY CULTURE

Among the newer areas of research in low achievement is the immediate family culture in which children grow up. Because low achievement has occurred in every society that schools its children, anthropologists have joined others in the social sciences to provide policy makers with insights that may be useful. Here's what the Council on Foundations has to say about their norms:

> Norms are the spoken and unspoken rules of cultures. Reinforced over time, they operate as invisible constraints on family members' behavior. Norms set standards for how family members dress, talk and act. They also set limits on what is permissible or impermissible behavior under different circumstances and conditions. More than just rules of etiquette, norms provide family members with a guide for living both within the home and without. [17]

A 1990 report from the US Department of Health and Human Services maintains,

> Based on various assumptions about what a strong family does, researchers have developed lists of structural and behavioral attributes that characterize successful families. In spite of differences in discipline and perspective, there seems to be a consensus about the basic dimensions of a strong, healthy family. The following constructs, which are often interrelated and complex, will be identified, defined, and described briefly as they exist in strong, healthy families:

- communication
- encouragement of individuals
- expressing appreciation

- commitment to family
- religious/spiritual orientation
- social connectedness
- ability to adapt
- clear roles
- time together[18]

All well and good, but for the nearly thirty years after this report, there are no government policies that address "strong, healthy families" and bear a connection to the implied recommendations of the Moynihan and Coleman reports in reducing black unemployment and strengthening black family structure. Strengthening single-parent homes wherever they exist is laudable, but these 1965 and 1966 reports saw single-parent families as a weakness, especially for black children, implying a need to reduce their numbers.[19]

Research on the achievement of children from single-parent homes versus those from two-parent homes is consistent. Children from two-parent families do better academically and in other respects. And the vast majority of African American children today are born to single mothers (about 70 percent). In his 2015 article on the Moynihan report, James Patterson concludes that the rise in fatherless families deeply disadvantages children, that it still remains risky for white writers to highlight black family problems, and that social science seems unable to develop a national family policy.[20]

Indeed, theoretical scholarship, let alone experimental research, on the "family" is lacking. Whatever is there has not led to effective policy or research. For example, a descriptive typology of "family cultures" emerged from a 2012 project at the University of Virginia, funded by the John Templeton Foundation.[21] There were no follow-up studies or policies; research on family culture has reached a dead end.

SCIENTIFIC AND PSYCHOLOGICAL RESEARCH ON ACADEMIC MOTIVATION

Ever-growing psychological research on academic motivation involves such characteristics as grit, tenacity, and perseverance.[22] Much of this research was stimulated by the 2007 book *Mindset: The New Psychology of Success* by psychologist Carol S. Dweck at Stanford University. To a large extent, the book is based on her own research, which dates back to the 1970s. Growth mindset and fixed mindset and their educational applications have attracted both praise and criticism.[23] (A growth mindset is the belief that intellectual abilities are not fixed but can be developed.)

There is also international research on the personality characteristics of low achievers.[24] However, it is not easy to modify anyone's personality, so researchers can only recommend that schools use guidance counselors judiciously.

The implications about mindsets (how students perceive their own abilities) are worrisome to many, and a cottage industry for growth mindset in the K–12 classroom has sprung up.[25] Despite criticism of the research on which Dweck's ideas rest and the mixed results from contemporary research on mindsets, the idea that there are either fixed or growth mindsets or mixtures of both is very appealing to many educators today. What parent can forget the *Little Engine That Could*? The little engine keeps saying, "I think I can, I think I can," and at the end, it achieves its goal. Most educators want their students to believe that their efforts matter, and they want their students to persist despite failure.[26]

Dweck's goal is a widely accepted educational one—learning—and she thinks her work will help to close the achievement gap.[27] As she explains, while "teachers who heap praise on students may assume they have adopted a growth mindset, . . . growth mindset is not about making low-achieving kids feel good in the moment but not learn in the long run."[28] She doesn't want excessive, artificial, or routine teacher praise to hide them.[29] Unfortunately, contemporary education jargon like "closing achievement gaps" is not helpful in defending her position.

Policy-making officials, not teachers or parents, have been obsessed with closing achievement gaps for decades. The Department of Education, the National Assessment of Educational Progress, and most state educational agencies regularly publish statistics based on state or national test scores showing that students in certain subgroups are consistently at the bottom of an academic skyscraper, compared with students in other subgroups. Is reinforcing a negative stereotype a healthy or educational thing to do? Years ago, most educators believed there would always be low achievers among us, even in most nineteenth-century schools outside the South, when most students were color-less statistically and had no particular ethnicity.

A goal of the original ESEA in 1965 was to strengthen public education and improve academic achievement in all students. The reduction or elimination of gaps is the goal of ESSA and the plans all states were required to submit to the Department of Education for review and approval if they wanted Title I money. Closing gaps is an educational goal that raises many questions about what teachers can do for students with a wide range of interests and reading levels. How exactly does a classroom teacher close gaps if she also is trying to improve academic achievement in all students in the class? She can't easily do both at the same time.

Critics of growth mindsets, such as education writer Alfie Kohn, fear that a too-strong a concern about teachers' ensuring their students have growth mindsets may lead them to offer their students false praise.[30] They don't want teachers repeating "Good job!" or "Good work!" to anything a student produces. Nor does Dweck want them to do that. However, some weak students do need a pat on the back occasionally. Reasonable parents and school administrators generally want teachers to give honest feedback to all students and help needy students with revising or correcting or moving ahead to a new challenge, not act like cheerleaders in a classroom. And it's possible, as at least one critic insists, that Kohn goes overboard in his criticism.[31]

How many teachers years ago told their students that a paper or quiz grade was good (or bad) because the student was naturally bright (or stupid)? Or, all that matters is effort? A strawman had to be constructed in order to make today's teachers pay attention to mindsets and consciously do or say something. Worse, this kind of pep talk has become one more of the many features of classroom pedagogy and curriculum that teachers are responsible for—along with low achievement. They are implicitly accused of encouraging fixed mindsets if their students don't show they learned Y for the federal- or state-mandated test of X, Y, and Z.

The pedagogical controversies about mindsets are related to motivation. In addition to introducing parents and educators to more educational jargon or edu-babble, they raise questions about something all teachers and parents understand: Some students appear eager or ready to learn no matter what the subject is, while others show interest only for a limited range of time and topics, if any.

A 2009 typology of reasons for low motivation in low achievers provides an interesting insight for educators. Psychologist Steven Reiss wanted to research the motives behind poor academic achievement. He offers six motivational reasons for low achievement in schools and believes that each has its own intervention: (1) fear of failure (or a high need for acceptance), (2) incuriosity (a low need for cognition), (3) lack of ambition (a low need for power), (4) spontaneity (a low need for order), (5) lack of responsibility (a low need for honor), and (6) combativeness (a high need for vengeance).[32] What is especially useful in Reiss's typology today is the implication that many low achievers are strongly motivated in directions other than schooling. Not all children want to spend much or most of their nonschool time reading or writing. That doesn't mean there is something wrong with them.

Some scientists have developed a very different approach to understanding motivation in relation to low achievement. In a study published in 2008, medical and other scientific researchers tried to work out the neural basis for the motivation for academic achievement. They explain what they found in imagery (MRIs) of brain activity in young people who had the motivation to learn compared to the brain activity of those who wanted to gain monetary rewards: "We compared the activation in the brain obtained during reported high states of motivation for learning with the ones observed when the motivation was based on monetary reward."[33] The authors do not suggest educational implications based on the differences they found in brain activity, but the idea of motivating K–12 students with monetary rewards has been around for a long time.

Some philanthropists and others long ago began to consider the promise of monetary rewards in college to incentivize academic learning and going to college for low-income students. Unfortunately, the research wasn't designed well, so evaluations of I Have a Dream efforts to encourage low achievers in K–12 to study harder, complete high school, and go to college via free college tuition are inconclusive.[34]

As indicated on the What Works Clearinghouse website (a service run by the Department of Education),

> I Have A Dream is a program that encourages students in low-income communities to complete high school and go on to college. The program guarantees that tuition for higher education will be covered after high school graduation. . . . The WWC identified 14 studies of I Have A Dream that were published or released between 1988 and 2008. No studies of I Have A Dream that fall within the scope of the Dropout Prevention review protocol meet What Works Clearinghouse (WWC) evidence standards. The lack of studies meeting WWC evidence standards means that, at this time, the WWC is unable to draw any conclusions based on research about the effectiveness or ineffectiveness of I Have A Dream.[35]

Perhaps other ways to incentivize low-income students would have clearer and positive results. It may well be that the motivation to learn is difficult to identify, isolate, and stimulate. But the research on motivation has potential uses for many teachers and parents of young children if used sensibly, once there is a large enough and well-designed body of such research to permit conclusions and recommendations.

SUMMARY

There is little experimental research on changes in family-related factors that might improve children's academic achievement. But other noneducation areas of research have attracted the attention of education policy makers. This broad range of noneducation research on low achievement underscores the interest in low achievers (who are often but not always low-income students). It also suggests that many researchers across many disciplines, like publishers and test developers, pay attention to trends and funding sources in educational policies and issues. But so far, no useful insights for addressing low achievement have emerged.

KEY IDEAS TO REMEMBER

1. Noneducation researchers have looked at such issues as (1) technologies used in and out of school, (2) adolescent sleep needs, (3) school discipline, (4) poverty, (5) family culture, and (6) academic motivation.
2. Noneducation researchers, such as scientists, medical professionals, anthropologists, sociologists, and lawyers, have explored non-teacher-related aspects of students' lives and suggest possible factors affecting student achievement that warrant educators' attention.
3. Much of the research by noneducation researchers has looked at factors affecting most students, not just low achievers. So far, studies have produced no useful insights for K–12 educators to address low achievement.

NOTES

1. Henrietta Cook, "'It Was Creepy': The Parents Option Out of Technology in the Classroom," *Age*, August 25, 2018, https://www.theage.com.au/national/victoria/it-was-creepy-the-parents-opting-out-of-technology-in-the-classroom-20180825-p4zzqf.html.

2. Shiva Ainloo, "Affirmative 4—'A New Study Shows That Students Learn Way More Effectively from Print Textbooks than Screens," *Textbooks or Tablets* (blog), November 14, 2017, https://textbooksortablets.wordpress.com/category/affirmative-arguments.

3. Benjamin Herold, "Technology in Education: An Overview," *Education Week*, February 5, 2016, https://www.edweek.org/ew/issues/technology-in-education/index.html.

4. Swiss Tropical and Public Health Institute, "Mobile Phone Radiation May Affect Memory Performance in Adolescents, Study Finds," *ScienceDaily*, July 19, 2018, www.sciencedaily.com/releases/2018/07/180719121803.htm.

5. Susan Patrick and Allison Powell, *A Summary of Research on the Effectiveness of K–12 Online Learning* (Vienna, VA: International Association for K–12 Online Learning, June 2009), https://www.k12.com/sites/default/files/pdf/school-docs/NACOL_ResearchEffectiveness-hr.pdf.

6. Federal Bureau of Investigation, "Education Technologies: Data Collection and Unsecured Systems Could Pose Risks to Students," public service announcement, September 13, 2018, https://www.ic3.gov/media/2018/180913.aspx.

7. Jessica C. Levenson, "Adolescent Sleep and Media Use," Children's Hospital of Pittsburgh, September 12, 2017, http://childrenspgh.org/adolescent-sleep-and-media-use/.

8. Judith A. Owens, "School Start Times for Adolescents," *Pediatrics* 134, no. 3 (2014): 642–49, http://pediatrics.aappublications.org/content/pediatrics/early/2014/08/19/peds.2014-1697.full.pdf.

9. Owens, "School Start Times."

10. Chaelin K. Ra, Junhan Cho, Matthew D. Stone, Julianne De La Cerda, Nicholas I. Goldenson, Elizabeth Moroney, Irene Tung, Steve S. Lee, and Adam M. Leventhal, "Association of Digital Media Use with Subsequent Symptoms of Attention-Deficit/Hyperactivity Disorder among Adolescents," *Journal of the American Medical Association* 320, no. 3 (2018): 255–63, https://jamanetwork.com/journals/jama/article-abstract/2687861; Leonard Sax, "Does Too Much Screen Time Really Cause ADHD?" *Psychology Today*, September 6, 2018, https://www.psychologytoday.com/us/blog/sax-sex/201809/does-too-much-screen-time-really-cause-adhd.

11. "Lawsuits Undermine School Discipline, Hinder Education, Argues NYU Education Professor in New Book to Be Launched at Sept. 29 Book Signing," press release, New York University, September 25, 2003, https://www.nyu.edu/about/news-publications/news/2003/september/lawsuits_undermine_school.html.

12. John R. Martin, "School Discipline and Disparate Impact," *Engage* 13, no. 1 (2012), https://fedsoc.org/commentary/publications/school-discipline-and-disparate-impact.

13. Martin, "School Discipline."

14. Evie Blad, "School Discipline Debate Central to Hearing for Trump Civil Rights Nominee," *Education Week*, December 5, 2017, http://blogs.edweek.org/edweek/rulesforengagement/2017/12/school_discipline_debate_central_to_hearing_for_trump_civil_rights_nominee.html; Mary Byrne, "Ill-Advised Opposition to Rescindment of Fed School Discipline Guidance," Truth in American Education, August 29, 2018, https://truthinamericaneducation.com/federalized-education/ill-advised-opposition-to-rescindment-of-fed-school-discipline-guidance; Nora Gordon, *Disproportionality in Student Discipline: Connecting Policy to Research* (Washington, DC: Brookings Institute, 2018), https://www.brookings.edu/research/disproportionality-in-student-discipline-connecting-policy-to-research; Claudia Rowe, "Race Dramatically Skews Discipline, Even in Elementary School," *Seattle Times*, June 23, 2015, updated March 18, 2016, https://www.seattletimes.com/education-lab/race-dramatically-skews-discipline-even-in-elementary-school.

15. Richard Rothstein, "Does 'Poverty' Cause Low Achievement?" *Working Economics* (blog), October 8, 2013, https://www.epi.org/blog/poverty-achievement.

16. Leila Morsy and Richard Rothstein, *Five Social Disadvantages That Depress Student Performance* (Washington, DC: Economic Policy Institute, 2015), https://www.epi.org/publication/five-social-disadvantages-that-depress-student-performance-why-schools-alone-cant-close-achievement-gaps.

17. "The Effects of Family Culture on Family Foundations," Council on Foundations, 2019, https://www.cof.org/content/effects-family-culture-family-foundations.

18. Maria Krysan, Kristin A. Moore, and Nicholas Zill, *Research on Successful Families* (Washington, DC: US Department of Health and Human Services, 1990), https://aspe.hhs.gov/basic-report/research-successful-families.

19. Wikipedia Contributors, "African American Family Structure," *Wikipedia*, updated February 11, 2019, https://en.wikipedia.org/wiki/African-American_family_structure.

20. James T. Patterson, "Moynihan and the Single-Parent Family," *EducationNext* 15, no. 2 (Spring 2015), http://educationnext.org/moynihan-and-the-single-parent-family.

21. Carl Desportes Bowman, *Culture of American Families: A National Survey* (Charlottesville, VA: Institute for Advanced Studies in Culture, 2012), https://s3.amazonaws.com/iasc-prod/uploads/pdf/4a18126c1a07680e4fbe.pdf; James Davison Hunter, "Four Family Cultures of America Identified," *ScienceDaily*, November 15, 2012, www.sciencedaily.com/releases/2012/11/121115152546.htm.

22. Tina Barseghian, "How to Foster Grit, Tenacity and Perseverance: An Educator's Guide," *Mindshift*, February 20, 2013, https://www.kqed.org/mindshift/27212/how-to-foster-grit-tenacity-and-perseverance-an-educators-guide.

23. Carol Dweck, "Growth Mindset Interventions Yield Impressive Results," *Mindset Scholars Network* (blog), June 26, 2018, http://mindsetscholarsnetwork.org/carol-dweck-responds-recent-criticisms-growth-mindset-research/#; Coert Visser, "Criticisms of Mindset Research," *Progress-Focused Approach* (blog), January 15, 2017, http://www.progressfocused.com/2017/01/criticisms-of-mindset-research.html.

24. Mariam Adawiah Dzulkifli and Intan Aidura Alias, "Students of Low Academic Achievement—Their Personality, Mental Abilities and Academic Performance: How Counsellor Can Help?" *International Journal of Humanities and Social Science* 2, no. 23 (December 2012): 220–25, http://www.ijhssnet.com/journals/Vol_2_No_23_December_2012/25.pdf.

25. Katie Finley, "4 Ways to Encourage a Growth Mindset in the Classroom," EdSurge, October 24, 2014, https://www.edsurge.com/news/2014-10-24-4-ways-to-encourage-a-growth-mindset-in-the-classroom.

26. "Growth Mindset," Glossary of Education Reform, August 29, 2013, https://www.edglossary.org/growth-mindset/.

27. David Glenn, "Carol Dweck's Attitude," *Chronicle of Higher Education*, May 9, 2010, https://www.chronicle.com/article/Carol-Dwecks-Attitude/65405.

28. John Fensterwald, "There's More to a 'Growth Mindset' than Assuming You Have It," *EdSource*, November 23, 2015, https://www.huffingtonpost.com/entry/growth-mindset_us_565f315de4b072e9d1c455d4.

29. Carol Dweck, "Carol Dweck Revisits the 'Growth Mindset,'" *Education Week*, September 22, 2015, https://www.edweek.org/ew/articles/2015/09/23/carol-dweck-revisits-the-growth-mindset.html.

30. Alfie Kohn, "The Perils of 'Growth Mindset' Education: Why We're Trying to Fix Our Kids When We Should Be Fixing the System," *Salon*, August 16, 2015, https://www.salon.com/2015/08/16/the_education_fad_thats_hurting_our_kids_what_you_need_to_know_about_growth_mindset_theory_and_the_harmful_lessons_it_imparts.

31. Coert Visser, "Alfie Kohn's Misleading Critique of Carol Dweck," *Progress-Focused Approach* (blog), August 21, 2015, http://www.progressfocused.com/2015/08/alfie-kohns-misleading-critique-on.html.

32. Steven Reiss, "Six Motivational Reasons for Low School Achievement," *Child and Youth Care Forum* 38, no. 4 (August 2009): 219–25, http://www.idspublishing.com/resources/6published%20reasons.pdf.

33. Kei Mizuno, Masaaki Tanaka, Akira Ishii, Hiroki C. Tanabe, Hirotaka Onoe, Norihiro Sadato, and Yasuyoshi Watanabe, "The Neural Basis of Academic Achievement Motivation," *NeuroImage* 42, no. 1 (August 2008): 369–78, https://www.sciencedirect.com/science/article/pii/S1053811908006083.

34. "I Have a Dream," What Works Clearinghouse, March 2009, https://ies.ed.gov/ncee/wwc/Docs/InterventionReports/wwc_ihaveadream_031009.pdf.

35. "I Have a Dream." According to its website, "WWC reviews existing research on different programs, products, practices, and policies in education. Its goal is to provide educators with the information they need to make evidence-based decisions."

Chapter Six

Why Philanthropists Have Wasted Money on Low-Achieving Schools

The number of philanthropists eager to do something for public education is growing.[1] At a March 2018 meeting of more than 150 philanthropists, the conclusion was "to double down on quality: Strengthen the teacher pipeline, strengthen curriculum, fund wraparound services."[2] This was a puzzling conclusion because, in his review of the research on wraparound services one month earlier, Matt Barnum had reported, "Research shows that these efforts often do help learning, but in a number of cases they don't seem to have any effect—and it's not clear why efforts sometimes succeed and sometimes don't."[3] Apparently, the philanthropists at the March meeting had not read the reporter's February article or didn't care what he had found in his review of the research; they had money to spend. Barnum has also told the readers of his February 2018 article. "There appears to be stronger evidence for the academic benefits of direct anti-poverty programs that are separate from schools. The earned income tax credit, health insurance, child tax credit, food stamps, and simply giving cash to low-income families have all been linked to better outcomes in schools for children."[4] Were any philanthropists interested in programs strengthening low-income families? The reporter gives no indication of such an interest among any of the philanthropists at the March meeting, nor does Barnum provide references to studies on the academic benefits of antipoverty programs independent of school initiatives. In this chapter, I present the results of recent philanthropic projects for low-performing students. I also note concerns about the lack of accountability in philanthropy for education.

WHERE EXTRA FUNDS FOR LOW-PERFORMING
SCHOOLS COME FROM

A large proportion of the extra funds going to schools with many low achievers (often called "low-performing schools") has come from Title I in the Elementary and Secondary Education Act (ESEA) since its inception in 1965 and from federal school-improvement grants (SIGs) for "turnover" or "transformational" models of school change.[5] Judging from the results of tests for the Nation's Report Cards, this large pot of taxpayer money has accomplished little for low achievers. The chief beneficiaries seem to have been the consultants and companies that schools were pressured into using (for SIGs) in order to satisfy federal requirements. That is what the Arkansas Bureau of Legislative Research concluded in its February 2012 report after looking at results in Arkansas and the amount of money the state got in the form of a SIG.[6]

As the bureau notes, with access to new and greatly enhanced (federal) funding and with intense pressure to pull up test scores, school districts found themselves facing an "aggressive school improvement consulting industry vying for their business."[7] The bureau further notes that many school-improvement companies started out providing professional development and gradually began to offer more comprehensive services as more federal school-improvement funding became available. It would seem that, at least in the case of the companies selling services in Arkansas, their eagerness to tap the money stream made available by the federal government outstripped the effectiveness of the services they sold the state.

Low-performing schools receive taxpayer money from all three levels of government. Most of the federal money sent to states and local school districts is for children of low-income families. Around 10 percent of the funds that low-performing schools receive today comes from the federal government, but exactly how much the federal government sends to the states for education is not readily available.[8]

About another 45 percent of the funds for all public K–12 schools in a state come from state taxpayers. Another 45 percent of taxpayer money for public K–12 schools in a state comes from local taxpayers. A figure for extra state and local funds sent to low-performing schools beyond what a school district with no children from low-income families receives is not available. There is consensus that it costs more to educate poor children than middle-class children in the suburbs, but it is unclear what the additional costs are for. Smaller classes? More teachers per pupil? More supervisors per pupil or per teacher?

Extra taxpayer money for low-performing schools has come from formula-based appropriations by state legislatures trying to compensate large urban districts for an increasing loss of residential-property-based tax revenues despite the increase in the tax rate for commercial properties. In most communities, commercial properties are generally taxed at a higher rate than residential properties, but there are limits to what can be squeezed from a golden goose—or a sitting duck, as the case may be. Most states have state income taxes as well as sales taxes. Some state legislatures have been able to allocate some of the revenues they collect from sales or income taxes (or state-run lotteries) to school districts with high numbers of students from low-income families. But unless it is made clearer what urban educators should be spending money on to make a difference for low achievers, those wells may soon dry up or waste a lot more money.

PHILANTHROPISTS WITH DEEP POCKETS AND LITTLE TO SHOW FOR THEM

Some of the extra funds to *low-performing* schools (beyond local, state, and federal grants or appropriations) have come as gifts from very wealthy individuals or foundations. For example, Walter Annenberg gave $500 million in the 1990s (matched by more than $600 million) to many schools, while Mark Zuckerberg gave $100 million (matched by another $100 million) to Newark, New Jersey, in 2010. The total grants to schools and projects related to the Common Core from the Bill and Melinda Gates Foundation (including Warren Buffett's $30 billion to the Gates Foundation) can't be calculated easily, but it is likely many billions. There is a wide range of other large donors, from Eli Broad and the Walton family to the Laura and John Arnold Foundation. There are also many donors of smaller amounts.[9] Details on specific amounts given by wealthy individuals in various locations across the country can be found in an investigative report by the Network for Public Education Action, "Hijacked by Billionaires: How the Super Rich Buy Elections to Undermine Public Schools."[10]

Early grants, such as the Annenberg money, had few strings attached.[11] But, like all the others, it accomplished little for students academically, although personnel in the various projects did well monetarily, according to reporters. The earliest Title I funds amounted to billions; required little more than an audit to ensure the schools spent the money in approved categories; and, like the philanthropists' grants, accomplished little, judging from the Nation's Report Cards.

More recent grants, like Zuckerberg's gift to Newark, have had strings attached but no higher rate of effectiveness. Although some articles imply there were positive results, there are more reports criticizing than praising how the money was handled. EdSurge concludes about the lack of significant results for the students in Newark in 2017, "'Everyone's getting paid, but Raheem still can't read.' That was one of the most memorable and scathing quotes in "The Prize," Dale Russakoff's investigation into how the $200

million given to Newark Public Schools by Mark Zuckerberg and other donors in 2010 was spent. The general impression, at the time of the book's
release in 2015, was: not very well."[12]

In contrast, a study funded by the Chan-Zuckerberg Initiative, led by
Harvard and Dartmouth researchers and released about the same time, found
statistically significant gains in Newark students' achievement in English but
not in math. However, a gain that is statistically significant is not necessarily
practically significant (e.g., students may have gotten eight problems right
instead of seven on a short post-test). And the use of large numbers of
students in a study makes it easier for evaluators to find a statistically significant gain. This study managed to find a very small pot of gold at the end of
the Newark rainbow, but how it did so is informative:

> In 2011–12, Newark launched a set of educational reforms aided by $200
> million in private philanthropy. Using data from 2009 through 2016, we evalu-
> ate the change in Newark students' achievement growth relative to similar
> students and schools elsewhere in New Jersey. We measure achievement
> growth using a "value-added" model, controlling for prior achievement, demo-
> graphics and peer characteristics. By the fifth year of reform, Newark saw
> statistically significant gains in English and no significant change in math
> achievement growth. . . . Shifting enrollment accounted for 62 percent of the
> improvement in English. In math, such shifts offset what would have been a
> decline in achievement growth. [13]

The money Zuckerberg gave Newark falls into four broad categories:

1. Labor and contract costs: $89.2 million
2. Charter schools: $57.6 million
3. Consultants: $21 million
4. Various local initiatives: $24.6 million

It is clear that "consultants" made a lot of money for whatever they did.
Interestingly, among them were Student Assessment Partners, a company led
by writers of Common Core's standards, along with an organization called
Achieve the Core, designed to help Newark's teachers to address the standards that Common Core's writers had themselves created.[14] No questions
were raised about possible conflicts of interest. Newark teachers did not
make extra money out of the various projects set into motion by Zuckerberg's money.[15] Overall, the goal that Zuckerberg set out to achieve—to
enact reforms that would make Newark a model city for education reform—
is considered a failure.[16]

Another long-term study, financed directly by the Gates Foundation,
clearly bit the dust according to its evaluators—the Rand Corporation and the
American Institutes for Research. This multiyear study (2009–2015) on

teacher effectiveness sought to find out what kinds of teacher evaluations led to increased student achievement.[17] There was no significant impact on student achievement in either math or reading, despite the fact that the study cost Gates multimillions and had considerable buy-in from participating school systems.

PHILANTHROPIST GIFTS AS LEVERAGE FOR PUBLIC MONEY

The Gates Foundation has given much more money to education than any other charitable agency or foundation. Its officials are aware that much of what it gives the schools must serve as leverage to get taxpayers' money to take over for the indefinite life of the projects it has created and funded. If there is no public money from local or state taxpayers to match or supersede the private money given to the schools, the projects that the foundation has created with the help of local educators will disappear, mainly because they weren't initially built into the local school budget or had no grassroots support or both.

How the Gates Foundation works with state or local education agencies is very different from the way philanthropists of yesteryear worked with state and local municipal agencies. Take, for example, the Carnegie grants for public library buildings in the late nineteenth and early twentieth centuries (1883–1929).[18] Not unreasonably, the Carnegie grants were conditioned on towns and cities ensuring part of the cost of operations, maintenance, and repairs. Interestingly, according to one source, Carnegie made no provision for the key asset of libraries—books—causing some communities to reject his library offers because of concerns that they couldn't generate or maintain a collection.[19] (There was, however, some opposition related to Carnegie's politics.)

Carnegie's well-known conditions were similar across communities and straightforward, and civic officials had to state their compliance in a formal letter (probably available to the public). First, the municipality would provide a suitable building site. Second, the municipal council would appropriate by taxation no less than 10 percent of the grant amount to annually support library operations. In addition, Carnegie grants were given only to public libraries that were open to citizens free of charge without membership fees.

There aren't striking differences between the conditions for local library grants established by a nineteenth-century philanthropist and the conditions for education grants established by today's leading philanthropists. But there *are* differences, as Richard Lee Colvin, later head of the Hechinger Institute, notes: "Many [philanthropists] are personally involved in overseeing the grants they give, and they insist on results from educators and schools. They believe good leadership, effective management, compensation based on performance, competition, the targeting of resources, and accountability for results can all pay dividends for education as well as for foundations."[20]

Today's philanthropists not only tend to want results (not unreasonable), but they also seem to want them mostly in the form of test scores—something quantifiable. In contrast, Carnegie didn't ask for regular increases in the number of patrons using a public library his money built or regular increases in the number of books borrowed. Of course, the qualities mentioned by Colvin matter (e.g., good leadership). No local school board or administration would dismiss any of them, although they might wonder how to compensate teachers based on performance. But local school boards and local educators might wonder why test results seem to be all that matter because the phenomenon of "teaching to the test" has long been known as a corrupting influence on teachers and schools.[21]

Unfortunately, foundations and the Department of Education haven't come up with anything other than test-based accountability. Performance-based assessments are now being promoted to assess "personalized learning." But they are one of the costliest types of assessment ever developed, as Kentucky educators learned in the 1990s when trying to use student portfolios.[22] "Authentic assessment," as it was referred to then (to some extent for rhetorical purposes), was also slow, cumbersome, subjective, and unreliable, as commentators point out in Jay Mathews's 2004 article on the topic.[23] So far, foundations, including the Gates Foundation, are not promising to pay for "performance-based assessments."

Despite the major problem most philanthropists have faced in their efforts to reform public education—notably community resistance to their ideas about reform—Colvin still concludes that there is reason for hope. Philanthropists are funding outside evaluations, and "they seem to be more transparent and forthright about the shortcomings of what they're funding as well as their successes."[24]

Transparency is a worthy objective, but it is doubtful that parents are consoled when finding out that their children lost a year or more of academic schooling after the fact, if their children had no choice but to participate in a philanthropist's education initiative, especially if the philanthropist's own children or grandchildren were in private schools known for an effective academic curriculum. The bigger problem is the mounting criticism of the impact of big philanthropists on education as philanthropy to education is increasing.[25] Investments that significantly alter public institutions can create sustainability issues if funders' priorities shift and private support is withdrawn. One example is the Bill and Melinda Gates Foundation's withdrawal from its small-schools initiatives, which left districts to fund schools that were more expensive to run than larger schools.

Today a very wealthy philanthropist is interested in his own ideas about preschool programs. In late 2018, Jeff Bezos, founder of Amazon, announced that he would invest several billions in preschool programs for "underserved" children.[26] He also announced that these preschool programs would be "Montessori-inspired." What that means was not clarified, nor does he explain how he decided that these children needed a Montessori-inspired preschool program. Does he know that Montessori-trained teachers are required for Montessori schools (and that there is an American version, as well as a European version, of a Montessori school)? As the meeting of philanthropists in March had made clear, their biggest problem was that foundations come in with ideas that a community hasn't bought into yet. Philanthropists must question if what their foundations offer works on the scale they fund with the children in question and if it is something that can be taught with desired results by trained American teachers.

MOTIVES OF PHILANTHROPISTS

Very wealthy philanthropists traditionally have often been very good businessmen. But they rarely had teaching or school administrative experience. And few, if any, were like John D. Rockefeller, who hired a minister to help him dispose of his wealth. Today's philanthropists in education can hire whomever they want as consultants, but judging from the ineffectiveness of their specific projects in the past several decades, they have a penchant for hiring people who have never accomplished much in the schools but must know how to sell their ineffective ideas to those who fund them. Think about the names of the people associated with the Gates Foundation's projects in the schools. Is there one that stands out for having accomplished something in higher education or in the schools and at a smaller scale before promoting a large-scale project? As a teacher? As an administrator? As a curriculum developer?

So why do well-heeled philanthropists give money for projects or programs that claim they will turn low-achieving students from low-income families into high school graduates or college material, especially when they must know in advance that the chance for accomplishing much in education is close to zero? Regardless of philanthropists' motives, the costs to the public at large and to schoolchildren and their parents may be huge and not easily repaid.

We know little about the motives of philanthropists, and it is not easy to determine real from professed motives. For example, it is well known that Andrew Carnegie was self-educated. He also wrote, "It was from my own early experience that I decided there was no use to which money could be applied so productive of good to boys and girls who have good within them and ability and ambition to develop it, as the founding of a public library in a community."[27] It is true that, until the middle of the nineteenth century, most libraries in this country were private athenaeums or private collections. It is possible that Carnegie's interest in funding the building of public libraries stemmed from his childhood experiences, but how can anyone be sure even if he said so? Does it matter? Do we know why Eli Broad, whose money was made from real estate development, has focused on public education? Or why Bill and Melinda Gates, who never went to public schools and don't send their children to any, focus on public education? Or why Jeff Bezos decided to focus on preschool programs?

Let me offer a tongue-in-cheek hypothesis: It looks good when one stands before the pearly gates of heaven and shows that he gave a lot of his money to benefit the "unwashed" of the world. And, it may make one stand out in front of those big gates, if she can show that she gave away even more of her own money than other billionaires did. In the Pacific Northwest, among some native groups, one's accumulated wealth—in blankets or fish or canoes—was often thrown onto a big fire as a way to celebrate an occasion.[28] In other words, big-time philanthropy in education may be a form of "potlatching," a way to show off one's wealth by throwing it away.

SUMMARY

Maybe philanthropists get better press when they give money directly for the benefit of poor children or their schools, even if they don't get the results they hope for. Maybe they get better press when they can lock into their schemes an endless flow of taxpayers' money, regardless of results? It's called leverage, and it's something that the federal government also aims for when it can.

As NAEP test scores suggest (via the Nation's Report Cards), very little positive change in the achievement level of low-achieving students has resulted from private philanthropy in the past four decades. Among the many criticisms leveled at private efforts to address low achievement are several prominent ones: (1) Their strings evade public scrutiny and discussion, leaving parents in the dark about the specific policies outside money has imposed on them; (2) they typically provide no accountability to local parents or the public at large; and (3) the private gifts are often intended as leverage for matching public funds but with little, if any, voter discussion or approval of the donor's specific intentions.[29] It's not apparent if the March 2018 meeting of philanthropists discussed these issues.

Similar charges could be made about federal policies embedded in the state plans required under the Every Student Succeeds Act (ESSA), passed by the House and Senate in 2015. The authors of the 2015 reauthorization of ESEA are unknown, as well as how much they were paid to write a bill more than one thousand pages long.

In addition to the criticisms on accountability, there are few independent evaluations of the projects that were funded. To its credit, the Gates Foundation had its multiyear project on teacher effectiveness evaluated by the Rand Corporation and the American Institutes for Research, and to their credit they got feedback from teachers and administrators in the project. But few studies include the results of anonymous surveys of participating teachers and administrators, if there are any such surveys. One would expect the most informed and insightful comments on curriculum changes and testing effects to come from a range of participating teachers and administrators who have been in one system long enough and taught enough students to understand how K–12 teaching and learning take place.

KEY IDEAS TO REMEMBER

1. An increasing number of philanthropists are interested in giving money for education.
2. So far, the initiatives philanthropists have funded have not succeeded in raising the academic achievement of low achievers.
3. Philanthropists today want specific results from their donations to education (like higher scores on state tests) that are beyond the control of teachers or administrators.
4. Philanthropists do not understand why there is little buy-in from parents and teachers for the reforms they want.
5. Most parents and voters know that today's philanthropists use as consultants for education projects people who have themselves never created or managed effective programs and policies in K–12 education.

NOTES

1. Editorial Board, "Gates Foundation Failures Show Philanthropists Shouldn't Be Setting America's Public School Agenda," *Los Angeles Times*, June 1, 2016, http://www.latimes.com/opinion/editorials/la-ed-gates-education-20160601-snap-story.html.
2. Caroline Bauman, "Big Education Funders Were in Memphis This Week. Here's What They Talked About," Chalkbeat, March 9, 2018, https://www.chalkbeat.org/posts/tn/2018/03/09/big-education-funders-were-in-memphis-this-week-heres-what-they-talked-about.
3. Matt Barnum, "Do Community Schools and Wraparound Services Boost Academics? Here's What We Know," Chalkbeat, February 20, 2018, https://www.chalkbeat.org/posts/us/2018/02/20/do-community-schools-and-wraparound-services-boost-academics-heres-what-we-know.
4. Barnum, "Do Community Schools Boost Academics?"
5. "Education Department Announces School Improvement Grants for 16 States," US Department of Education, June 23, 2016, https://www.ed.gov/news/press-releases/education-department-announces-school-improvement-grants-16-states.
6. Comments from this February 2012 report can be found in Sandra Stotsky and Trae Holzman, "The Costs of Federal Intervention in Local Education: The Effectiveness of America's Choice in Arkansas," *Nonpartisan Education Review* 11, no. 2 (2015): 1–16, https://nonpartisaneducation.org/Review/Articles/v11n2.pdf.

7. Stotsky and Holzman, "Costs of Federal Intervention."

8. Mike Maciag, "How Much Do States Rely on Federal Funding?" Governing, May 22, 2017, http://www.governing.com/topics/finance/gov-state-budgets-federal-funding-2015-2018-trump. html.

9. Rafael Heller, "Big Money and Its Influence on K–12 Education: An Interview with Sarah Reckhow," *Phi Delta Kappan* 99, no. 8 (2018): 41–45, http://www.kappanonline.org/heller-sarah-reckhow-k12-education-funding-foundations-big-money.

10. *Hijacked by Billionaires: How the Super Rich Buy Elections to Undermine Public Schools* (New York: Network for Public Education Action, September 2018), http://npeaction. org/wp-content/uploads/2018/09/Hijacked-by-Billionaires.pdf.

11. Ed Lasky, "More on the Annenberg Challenge," American Thinker, August 21, 2008, https://www.americanthinker.com/blog/2008/08/more_on_the_annenberg_challeng.html.

12. "Newark Students See Modest Gains from Mark Zuckerberg's $100M Gift," EdSurge, October 17, 2017, https://www.edsurge.com/news/2017-10-17-newark-students-see-modest-gains-from-mark-zuckerberg-s-100m-gift.

13. Mark J. Chin, Thomas J. Kane, Whitney Kozakowski, Beth E.Schueler, and Douglas O. Staiger, "School District Reform in Newark: Within- and Between-School Changes in Achievement Growth," National Bureau of Economic Research, Working Paper 23992, October 2017, https://cepr.harvard.edu/files/cepr/files/newark_ed_reform_nber_w23992_suggested_changes.pdf.

14. Achieve the Core, https://achievethecore.org.

15. Terry Gross, "Assessing the $100 Million Upheaval of Newark's Public Schools," *Fresh Air*, National Public Radio, September 21, 2015, https://www.npr.org/2015/09/21/442183080/assessing-the-100-million-upheaval-of-newarks-public-schools.

16. Abby Jackson, "Mark Zuckerberg's $100 Million Donation to Newark Public Schools Failed Miserably—Here's Where It Went Wrong," *Business Insider*, September 25, 2015, https://www.businessinsider.com/mark-zuckerbergs-failed-100-million-donation-to-newark-public-schools-2015-9.

17. "Gates' Teacher Effectiveness Initiative Fell Short, Study Finds," *Philanthropy News Digest*, July 2, 2018, http://philanthropynewsdigest.org/news/gates-teacher-effectiveness-initiative-fell-short-study-finds; Matthew A. Kraft, "What Have We Learned from the Gates-Funded Teacher Evaluation Reforms?" *EducationNext*, June 25, 2018, https://www.educationnext.org/learned-gates-funded-teacher-evaluation-reforms.

18. "Toronto's Carnegie Libraries," Toronto Public Library, 2018, https://www.torontopubliclibrary.ca/about-the-library/library-history/carnegie.jsp.

19. Annette Lamb, "Contemporary Libraries: 1900s," History of Libraries, 2019, http://eduscapes.com/history/contemporary/1900.htm.

20. Richard Lee Colvin, "The New Philanthropists," *EducationNext* 5, no. 4 (Fall 2005): 34–41, https://www.educationnext.org/thenewphilanthropists.

21. "Instructive Ideas," *Academic Questions* 26, no. 3 (September 2016), https://www.nas. org/articles/fall_2016_academic_questions_instructive_ideas; Sandra Stotsky, "Testing Limits," *Academic Questions* 26, no. 3 (September 2016): 285–98, https://link.springer.com/article/10.1007/s12129-016-9578-4.

22. "Assessments," Kentucky Department of Education, October 18, 2018, https://education.ky.gov/AA/Assessments/Pages/default.aspx.

23. Jay Mathews, "Portfolio Assessment," *EducationNext* 4, no. 3 (Summer 2004): 73–75, https://www.educationnext.org/portfolio-assessment.

24. Colvin, "New Philanthropists."

25. Editorial Board, "Gates Foundation Failures."

26. Lauren Camera, "Will Bezos Heed Other Education Philanthropy Mistakes?" *US News and World Report*, September 14, 2018, https://www.usnews.com/news/education-news/articles/2018-09-14/will-bezos-heed-other-education-philanthropy-mistakes.

27. "Andrew Carnegie's Story," Carnegie Corporation of New York, 2015, https://www.carnegie.org/interactives/foundersstory/#!/.

28. John Tierney, "Tips from the Potlatch, Where Giving Knows No Slump," *New York Times*, December 15, 2008, https://www.nytimes.com/2008/12/16/science/16tierney.html.

29. *Hijacked by Billionaires*.

Chapter Seven

Why We Haven't Learned from Failed *or* Effective Policies and Programs

Philanthropists have been unable to understand why both top-down and bottom-up educational policies haven't worked. According to the research, almost nothing they have invested in nor the grants they have given to the schools or to state departments of education to increase academic achievement in low achievers or low-income students have had the clear results they expected or hoped for.

For example, reviewers found insufficient evidence in well-designed studies for evaluating the outcomes of I Have a Dream programs. One such program was part of the Ariel Education Initiative (described as a mentoring and tutoring program) that former US Secretary of Education Arne Duncan was associated with in Chicago before becoming head of the Chicago Public Schools in 1991.[1] These philanthropist-funded programs encouraged an entire age cohort of children in a low-income public-housing project or an entire grade level of students in a low-income public elementary school to complete high school and go on to college by guaranteeing higher-education tuition after high school graduation. The What Works Clearinghouse (WWC), managed by the US Department of Education, reviewed the fourteen studies of I Have a Dream programs released between 1988 and 2008 and found "No studies of I Have A Dream that fall within the scope of the Dropout Prevention review protocol meet WWC evidence standards. The lack of studies meeting WWC evidence standards means that, at this time, the WWC is unable to draw any conclusions based on research about the effectiveness or ineffectiveness of I Have A Dream."[2]

Not only have philanthropists been unable to get a clear picture of the I Have a Dream program they supported showing whether it got low achievers to go beyond second base in academic achievement, but also education researchers and policy makers at the Department of Education and in state departments of education have been unable to grasp simple truths. An unwavering focus on the presumed needs of low-achieving students for pre-K–16 (promoted by Department of Education regulations and policies), as well as constant testing of all students based on Common Core–aligned standards, with teachers held "accountable" for scores in varying degrees across states, have not increased the academic achievement of low-income students or low achievers on a national scale. Indeed, current policies of the Department of Education have stimulated movement in the opposite direction, judging from 2017–2018 average National Assessment of Educational Progress (NAEP) scores for low-achieving student groups and ACT's 2018 report on college readiness.[3]

There have been good results in individual schools over the years. In talks and articles to promote her book *Schools That Succeed: How Educators Marshal the Power of Systems for Improvement*, Karin Chenoweth urges a return to the research on effective schools and hopes researchers and educators can tease out the scalable factors that made these schools effective.[4] Chenoweth wants desperately to believe, as does Education Trust, the organization now sponsoring her, that all low-income children can become higher achievers if schools are organized in ways that result in effective instruction for all students—a way of begging the highly problematic question because there are not one or even two models of effectiveness that researchers can point to. Chenoweth believes that education policies since the 1966 Coleman report have assumed that schools can't reach some children and that many schools have chosen to "teach in ways that can keep some children from learning almost anything."[5] In her article, Chenoweth attributes this nasty charge to Ronald Edmonds, an education researcher on "effective schools."

There are several problems with her conclusions. The first problem is that no one has implied that schools can't help poor children—certainly not James Coleman in his report. That report, like Moynihan's 1965 report, simply posits that family background matters more than teachers and schools in explaining student achievement. But like most other writers on education, Chenoweth has nothing to say about ways to strengthen family background and puts the entire burden of "reform" on teachers and administrators in the schools.

A second problem is that it is very difficult for education writers like Chenoweth, education school faculty, staff in departments of education or public instruction, and the Department of Education to accept the fact that, in general, massive low achievement has not been *caused* by the schools that low achievers attend. It is understandable (to reasonable people) why teachers cannot solve a complex social problem they didn't create. In contrast, high achievement is usually a reflection of what *is* taught because teachers typically teach students in advanced classes what they don't know but are able to read and write about. It is easier to close gaps by lowering the ceiling; schools simply don't offer advanced courses or teach advanced material. Parents can do so on their own, which may explain the huge growth in homeschooling in recent years and the superiority of homeschooled students to public school students in reading.

A third problem is that it is poor teaching to give all students in an age or grade cohort instruction at the same pace, regardless of the level of their reading and writing skills, which is what supporters of current Department of Education–approved standards and state plans recommend. In all cohorts at any age, there are faster and slower learners, and experienced elementary teachers learn to adjust their instruction to their students' demonstrated capacity to absorb what is being taught and their speed in doing so. Because high school teachers do not teach in self-contained classrooms, as elementary and many middle school teachers do, high schools may offer different levels of the same course, letting students choose the pace they are willing to work at. American schools have spent more than a century trying to provide for differences in the learning pace of a wide range of students. If all can really be taught at the same pace, then we need to see the evidence from the Department of Education.

A fourth problem is that massive low achievement, so far as can be determined, hasn't been remedied by teachers and administrators, no matter how much money they have been given—the empirical cast to the problem. There have been schools here and there where low achievers seem to have improved. They are called "high-quality" or "high-performing" schools. (These are not exam schools.) But education policy makers have not been able to scale them up or clone their administrators. The vast bulk of low achievers will stay, relatively speaking, exactly where they are now—at the bottom—except that Asian Americans will likely keep pushing the bar higher and making the gaps between them and other groups (including whites) larger.

WE CAN LEARN FROM PROGRAMS SHOWING LITTLE STUDENT PROGRESS

Schools with chiefly low-income students or low achievers are considered high performing if their test results are higher than expected. One of their characteristics, we are told, is "excellence in teaching and leadership." According to a report on "strategies to improve low-performing schools" issued by the Center for American Progress in 2016, the phrase has been used by Roland Fryer, a prominent economist known for his attempt to inject successful charter school practices into "traditional" schools. [6] According to the center's report, the vast school-improvement program he helped to design in

2010 for Houston, Texas, "implemented the following best practices of high-performing charters" based on Fryer's research on effective schooling models: (1) data-driven instruction; (2) excellence in teaching and leadership; (3) culture of high expectations; (4) frequent and intensive tutoring, or so-called high-dosage tutoring; and (5) extended school day and year. The long-term results of Houston's massive Apollo program, which Fryer designed, have been described as "statistically significant" gains in mathematics but "negligible" gains in reading. Moreover, "high-dosage tutoring" seems to be the source of the mathematics gains.[7]

Houston's results left policy makers with a conundrum. Low achievers seemed to respond to intensive math tutorials (all Houston students had regular math classes; only some had tutorials, too). However, it wasn't clear that targeted and intensive tutoring could achieve more than immediate higher test results. In other words, tutoring didn't seem to lead to lasting gains in both reading and math.

There is another problem that Houston educators needed to consider. Rice University's evaluation report recommended not only more math tutorials but also tutorials in reading for the future. First, what could the statistical effectiveness of math tutorials in Houston tell teacher-preparation programs and professional developers to focus on? Second, statistical significance is not practical significance; in this study, statistical significance likely reflects the large number of students in the Apollo program. And teacher-preparation programs and professional development do not typically show teachers how to do tutorials in any subject. A master's degree program in remedial reading might show teachers how to do one-on-one clinical work in reading, but that is not the same thing as a tutorial in reading.

The evaluations of the Apollo program implicitly suggest one major way we could learn something from school district program failures, particularly when sympathetic professionals are unwilling to say outright that a program whose goal they liked produced few or negative results and wasn't worth continuing and instead they provide meaningless recommendations to follow up. There are no hints in the Apollo findings that there might be much higher scores or lasting results if the schools did X or Y or Z. But we would have learned more by asking teachers in the Houston schools in an anonymous survey if the project was worth continuing and under what conditions.

Because classroom teachers ultimately bear the burden of a new policy or project in education, they are apt to be honest about what worked well, what didn't, and what they would recommend for a continued project (if they had not been rewarded monetarily for participation). This wasn't done in Houston, but teachers in an unsuccessful program should work with outside, independent evaluators to let policy makers know why a policy or program was ineffective from their perspective. Parents and school administrators provide limited but useful supplementary information.

WE CAN'T LEARN MUCH FROM INADEQUATE ANALYSES OF POLICY AND PROGRAM FAILURES

We can find lessons to be learned from several specific education policy failures in *Failure Up Close: What Happens, Why It Happens, and What We Can Learn from It*. This book consists of nine chapters by a variety of writers, plus concluding remarks by its two editors, Jay P. Greene and Michael Q. McShane. This volume begins with a chapter on the flaws in "deferring to" expertise in education policy to address policy failures. One flaw is thinking that "expertise" includes "political wisdom." Not explored is what expertise, if any, do policy makers responsible for a failed education policy have and how they became policy makers (political appointment, election, experience).

Another chapter raises questions about how to judge projects that have many educational goals and don't succeed in all of them, such as the different uses of technology in the schools. Who should decide which goals or uses make the projects policy failures or policy successes, and how should this be measured? Yet another chapter discusses how psychology is taught in teacher-training programs and criticizes a focus on abstract theories, not empirical generalizations. Other chapters on policy failures address programs or policies that have already been killed, mostly by Congress or the Department of Education (e.g., school-improvement grants under Race to the Top, No Child Left Behind's goal of proficiency for all by 2014, and teacher evaluation via value-added measures derived from students' test scores).

Greene and McShane are correct to say that much can be learned from an analysis of a failed education policy. They assert that we can learn from policy failures and that a good part of the problem is the lack of criteria for judging them as failures. They also provide information on some failed education policies enacted at the federal or state level and why they can be considered failures.

What would be interesting to know is why these particular policies were adopted to begin with. What problems were they seen as answers to? What justified them? Why did education policy makers think these policies would be successful? Were better alternatives to the chosen policy available? What did policy makers think would happen in the schools? Were policy makers willing to revise controversial policies *in media res*, so to speak? Were they willing to listen to critics, especially parents and teachers (the two best sources of information on the kinks in a new program), and make adjustments? Why or why not? If an analysis provides no answers or information to set the stage for the analysis, then there may be little that can be learned from a failed policy.

An inadequate analysis of a policy failure may result from more than the authors' failure to provide adequate background information. In an essay on the Show-Me Institute in Missouri, Richard Phelps, a testing expert, points out how a policy could be misinterpreted and misimplemented because informational materials that raise questions about the goals and implementation of the problematic policy were withheld at the time of its development and adoption or during its implementation.[8]

Phelps also wrote about several other well-known organizations: Achieve, Inc.; Thomas B. Fordham Institute; Bellwether Education News; Council of Chief State School Officers; and National Governors Association.[9] He notes how these organizations collaborated with each other to promote the Common Core Initiative. Meanwhile, most state and local boards of education, educators, and parents were unaware that these organizations were funded in large part by one entity to promote adoption of the gap-closing standards, which governors and chairs of state boards of education were already committed to do. Educators, the media, and the public at large were told that using these standards would make all students college- and career-ready, and these organizations colluded with each other to dupe elected officials, educators, the media, and state boards of education into believing they were getting independent evaluations of the virtues of these standards. Without information on the sources supporting and criticizing the adoption of a failed policy, its analysis is inadequate.

WE DON'T LEARN MUCH FROM EFFECTIVE POLICIES OR PROGRAMS, EITHER

On the face of it, it would seem reasonable to believe that we could learn much from successful policies and programs, but we haven't done so in recent years for several possible reasons: (1) Policy makers and others may not learn from an effective policy or program if it doesn't reflect their teaching and learning philosophies. At issue is ideological compatibility with prior views. (2) Policy makers and others may not want to learn from an effective policy or program they had nothing to do with. At issue is personal investment or self-esteem. (3) Policy makers and others may not want to learn from an effective policy or program if they don't have a positive relationship with whoever implemented it. At issue are elements of personal vendettas.

The following are two relatively clear examples of policy makers failing to learn from effective policies and programs. In both cases, policy makers were the members of a state board of education and a governor. One is from California; the other, from Massachusetts. In both cases, state policy makers knew about their quality and results of their existing policies and programs at the time that Common Core's standards in mathematics and English language arts were being developed. The quality and effectiveness of their own policies, programs, and standards were ignored in favor of different policies and standards with no empirical or historical data to support them, which strongly suggests that state policy makers and political leaders made a deliberate choice of mediocre or ineffective standards, perhaps for federal money, or didn't know what they were voting for (a very different problem).

The philosophy behind the two existing sets of policies or programs should be clarified right away. Both sets came out of a period of "education reform" that maintained all students needed to make academic gains—not just low-income or low-achieving students. Legislation in these two states in the 1990s was intended to strengthen public education for all student groups, however they were defined. This philosophical position can be traced back to the position on the post–World War II reforms that were judged as necessary in education, culminating in 1958 in the National Defense Education Act (NDEA) and the so-called *Sputnik*-era programs and ending about 1970. Education reformers sought through NDEA institutes to strengthen the school curriculum for all, especially in mathematics, science, and foreign languages. World War II had shown how deficient American high school graduates were in those subjects and their application. The publication of *A Nation at Risk* in 1983 can also be traced to this philosophical position.

The existence of such a stance can also be found in the first Elementary and Secondary Education Act (ESEA), passed by Congress in 1965 as part of President Johnson's War on Poverty. Its purpose was "to strengthen and improve educational quality and educational opportunities in the Nation's elementary and secondary schools"[10] Many educators today have forgotten that an original goal of education reform was to strengthen schools for all students, not to "close gaps," as in the 2015 reauthorization of ESEA.

California

The major distinguishing feature of the 1997 California mathematics standards was the build-up in the K–7 mathematics curriculum to grade 8, where all students were expected to take an Algebra I course. At the high point of enrollment, in 2013, 67 percent of middle school students—58 percent in grade 8, and 9 percent in grade 7—were enrolled in Algebra I.[11] The increase in taking and passing Algebra I in grade 8 after 1997 enabled more students to get to precalculus or calculus courses in upper high school grades. The number of college-ready students in mathematics steadily rose from 16,000 to 31,000 between 2006 and 2013. From 1997 to 2014, the California State University system, which keeps complete records on admissions and remediation, found increasingly more qualified students, and freshman enrollment more than doubled, from around 26,000 to around 63,000. At the same time, remediation rates in mathematics dropped from 52 percent to 27 percent.

Until the adoption of Common Core's standards in 2010 and their implementation in 2014, California had used its own mathematics standards, written largely by faculty in the mathematics department at Stanford University. But as Williamson Evers and Ze'ev Wurman note, Common Core's standards in both mathematics and English language arts were adopted even though they were not benchmarked to the standards in high-achieving countries *despite claiming that this was so*.[12] Common Core's standards were less clear than California's 1997 standards, and they had significant gaps in content coverage. Many mathematicians attested to deficiencies in Common Core's mathematics standards.[13]

So, what happened? According to Evers and Wurman,

> In K–12 education, the gains of the previous 10–15 years—as reflected in large increases in students successfully taking Algebra I early, and in students taking more advanced math courses in high school—have been reversed. As worrisome is the fact that disadvantaged minorities (who made faster gains than the rest of the cohort before Common Core) are losing ground after Common Core at faster rates.[14]

Based on student answers to questions on the Standardized Testing and Reporting (STAR) and National Assessment of Educational Progress (NAEP) tests, enrollment in Algebra I in grade 8 was 16 percent in 1999; it rose to 59 percent by 2011 and plummeted to 19 percent in 2017.

Were California educators and political leaders concerned about a decline in Hispanic and African American enrollment in advanced mathematics (and science) courses in high school (see figure 7.1)? The California State University system announced in 2017 that it would allow some students to take mathematics classes other than intermediate algebra in 2018 to satisfy the general mathematics requirement needed for graduation.[15] The public expressed concern about the number of lower-achieving students who didn't complete college because passing the intermediate algebra course had become an "obstacle" for them and because algebra wasn't necessary for the non-STEM career paths they had chosen. California educators and elected political leaders wanted to ensure that more Hispanics and African Americans completed a community or state college degree program, but they seemed interested only in graduating more semieducated students from California colleges, not more mathematically capable students from California high schools.

Massachusetts

The final version of the first set of English language arts standards to emerge after the Massachusetts Education Reform Act (MERA 1993) encompassed two-year grade spans from grades 4 to12 (mandated by law). Dated 1997,

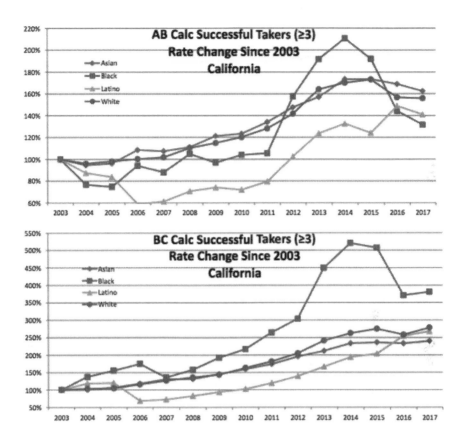

Figure 7.1.   Successful Takers of Calculus AB and BC in California Since 2003.
Source: Williamson M. Evers and Ze'ev Wurman, "California's Common Core Mistake," *Defining Ideas*, May 9, 2018. Available at https://www.hoover.org/research/californias-common-core-mistake.

these pre–Common Core standards highlighted oral language, vocabulary study, and the history of the English language and were preceded by an essay on teaching beginning reading skills and sample passages showing the level of reading expected by grade 4.[16] The 1997 Curriculum Framework *then* presented many standards for literary analysis, mainly for the four major types of genres (fiction, nonfiction, drama, poetry), followed by a smaller number of standards highlighting the "aims of discourse" for composition. Appendix A, vetted by the editors of the *Hornbook* (the major children's literature quarterly in the country), listed by educational level from kindergarten through grade 8 the *authors* reflecting our literary heritage and recommended authors only on the basis of the literary quality of their works. Appendix B listed authors for K–8 and 9–12 who mostly reflected contemporary movements worldwide. Most authors in appendix A were dead white and black authors of historical and cultural significance in American history. As they died, black and white American authors in appendix B were to be moved to appendix A.

Mainly authors' names were in both lists because high school English teachers in the Bay State wanted recommended authors, not titles (a few Nobel Prize–winning speeches by recognized writers were in the heritage list). Teachers said they preferred to choose for their classes the authors' works they thought were most appropriate to teach. A diverse range of literary scholars vetted both 9–12 lists. In a survey, these teachers anonymously rated on a scale of 1 to 5 the features of the new curriculum framework, including appendixes A and B. A clear majority approved the document's emphasis on literary texts. They helped to write the literature and writing standards and test items. Some English teachers selected appropriate passages and writing prompts for the state's ELA tests; reviewed the wording of the multiple-choice and open-response questions; rated student writing at all tested grade levels in holistic writing assessment sessions; and selected for the grades tested writing exemplars for the rating scale and annotated the revisions needed, which were posted on the department's website as teaching tools. The state's English teachers had some degree of ownership of the ELA standards and the tests based on them.

The Bay State's 2001 English language arts curriculum framework (a slight revision of the 1997 document, with grade-level standards added in 2004 to address the yearly testing requirements in grades 3–8 in No Child Left Behind) were judged as policy successes because students got high scores on independent tests that the state had no way to manipulate.

There were other criteria to use. When the state's department of education decided in 2005–2006 to revise the standards (because state standards had to be revised on a "timely" basis), a survey was sent out to the entire "field" (a traditional practice), asking English and reading teachers and related personnel for suggestions. Less than thirty anonymous responses were returned, and none came from practicing teachers. No one asked for changes in the standards themselves. The satisfaction of the state's English teachers with the 2001–2004 standards was clearly a sign of a policy success, even though department staff proceeded to make drastic changes in its first revised draft (possibly because of pressure from some education school faculty or the Department of Education).

But the standards alone were not the cause of student success in the Bay State. As of 2000, the state had new teacher licensing regulations and, in 2001, new professional-development criteria. The state's elementary teaching corps was also being strengthened in how to teach beginning reading (by means of Reading First workshops for in-service teachers and a stand-alone reading licensure test for prospective teachers), so students could better learn material addressing the new standards. Bay State students continue to be in first place on NAEP tests in 2018 (another criterion of policy success) because the quality of its teaching corps was strengthened in every K–12 subject, making for gains in all demographic groups. They are not in first place because of annual testing, as some have claimed, as annual testing in every subject came about only after the adoption of Common Core's standards in 2010.[17]

The best set of mathematics standards in Massachusetts to emerge after MERA 1993 was issued in 2000. It encouraged Algebra I in grade 8, but it didn't require it. The grade 8 test was mainly to address prealgebra material, even though about half of the grade 8 students in the state were already taking Algebra I. The document did list specific standards for traditional courses in Algebra I, Algebra II, geometry, and precalculus, so high school mathematics teachers could see what topics were expected to be covered if end-of-course tests were developed in high school.

California and Massachusetts were among the few states to provide standards for precalculus in their K–12 mathematics standards documents (though not assessed on state tests), a problem for Common Core's writers because its mathematics standards deliberately had no links from standards in earlier grades to calculus. In a September 2013 article, I quote lead Common Core mathematics writer Jason Zimba admitting at a state board of education public meeting, "If you want to take calculus your freshman year in college, you will need to take more mathematics than is in the Common Core."[18]

Unfortunately, Common Core's writers learned little, if anything, from the Bay State's pre–Common Core standards in both English language arts and mathematics, despite the claim that they learned a lot from them. Their effectiveness was clear by the time the writers, presumably chosen by the Gates Foundation, the Council for Chief State School Officers (CCSSO), and possibly Marc Tucker of the National Center on Education and the Economy (NCEE), were composing the Common Core standards for both subjects in 2009–2010. Bay State students had already placed first in three consecutive testing cycles on NAEP's tests in grades 4 and 8 in both mathematics and reading. In 2007, enrolled as a separate country, the Bay State placed sixth among the top countries in mathematics in grade 8 and tied for first place with Singapore in grade 8 science on Trends in International Mathematics and Science Study (TIMSS) and repeated the results in 2013.[19]

Nevertheless, in 2010, the Massachusetts Board of Education voted out its globally competitive standards in mathematics and English language arts seemingly for Race to the Top funds. Later, it revised its competitive science standards to be more compatible with those produced by Achieve, Inc. (Next Generation Science Standards, or NGSS), despite the fact that scientists heavily criticized Achieve's science standards for their inadequacies in mathematics (among other things).[20]

The question remains, Why did the Massachusetts Board of Education, supported by then-Governor Deval Patrick and Secretary of Education Paul Reville, vote out the only set of effective standards in English language arts and mathematics in the country? When personally asked that question in 2010, chair of the board Maura Banta, neither a mathematician nor a literary scholar, said that Common Core's standards had "higher expectations."[21]

Governor Charles Baker and Secretary of Education James Peyser (both since 2014), as well as most members of their state board of education, know relatively nothing about the relationship between high school science and mathematics—as little as Governor Patrick and Secretary of Education Reville knew—but they agreed to support less-rigorous standards in mathematics and science in the state plan in 2016. California educators and political leaders similarly agreed to adopt less-rigorous standards in science and mathematics in place of those that had been created by California-based academic experts and judged superior in academic quality by a range of experts to those in the rest of the country. There had already been much national talk of the need for more STEM-proficient students, but political leaders in Massachusetts as well as California chose to adopt inferior mathematics and science standards.

SUMMARY

How can we learn from a failed policy if those who were responsible won't admit that it failed? And how can we learn from effective policies when those who were responsible for voting them out or changing them won't explain in detail why they did so? These policy makers also can't show us effective policies and programs in their place. Members of the state boards of education that adopted Common Core's standards in 2010 or 2011 or the standards now in place have never explained publicly why they did so.

Did political leaders in any state in 2010–2011 really believe that skills-oriented standards would make low achievers college-ready, even though they were regularly told by mathematically illiterate reporters in the media and by organizations receiving funds from the Gates Foundation that these standards were rigorous? One state board of education (Kentucky) even agreed to adopt them before they were written, suggesting that it was more important to claim to address the problem (low achievement) with these standards than to actually strengthen public education for all. Or perhaps members of state boards really wanted less-rigorous standards for all students so that gaps could be closed.

One may easily wonder if that was the case because of the failure of state plans and the Department of Education to mention, never mind subscribe to, the latest ideas of E. D. Hirsch Jr., a distinguished literary scholar notably in favor of the Common Core at its inception. The title of his 2016 book from the Harvard Education Press says it all: *Why Knowledge Matters: Rescuing Our Children from Failed Educational Theories*. Its thrust is described on Amazon: "In the absence of a clear, common curriculum, Hirsch contends that tests are reduced to measuring skills rather than content."[22] And it is not as if *Education Week* didn't mention it. Reporter Liana Heitin also notes, "More than skills and strategies, students need knowledge."[23]

KEY IDEAS TO REMEMBER

1. No current policies or programs in education have been officially acknowledged as failures or in need of revision.
2. Partisans tend to describe only previous policies or programs developed by another party as failures or as deficient in their design.
3. Few policies in education are ever described as failures or successes because there are no generic solutions or silver bullets for any educational problem.
4. Congress does not ask why particular policies supported by the Department of Education are in place.
5. Think tanks, institutes, and other organizations that support education researchers may have withheld information contradicting the policies they supported as they were being formulated, adopted, or implemented.
6. Organizations that are funded by chiefly one entity may testify for each other's ideas on how to address a specific education policy, giving the appearance of independent corroboration.
7. Those who voted for policies affecting the academic content of the K–12 curriculum in general typically do not know much about what they are voting on and tend not to ask authentic academic experts for their professional judgment.

NOTES

1. National Basketball Association, "Participants: Arne Duncan," 2012 NBA All-Star Technology Summit: The New Internet, February 24, 2012, http://www.nba.com/techsummit/bio_arne_duncan.html.
2. "I Have a Dream," What Works Clearinghouse, March 2009, https://ies.ed.gov/ncee/wwc/Docs/InterventionReports/wwc_ihaveadream_031009.pdf.
3. *The Condition of College and Career Readiness, National 2018* (Iowa City: ACT, 2018), http://www.act.org/content/act/en/research/condition-of-college-and-career-readiness-2018.html.
4. Karin Chenoweth, "Reviving Research on Effective Schools," ResearchEd, September 26, 2018, https://researched.org.uk/reviving-research-on-effective-schools.
5. Chenoweth, "Reviving Research."
6. Chelsea Straus and Tiffany D. Miller, *Strategies to Improve Low-Performing Schools under the Every Student Succeeds Act* (Washington, DC: Center for American Progress, March 2016),

https://www.americanprogress.org/issues/education/reports/2016/03/02/132053/strategies-to-improve-low-performing-schools-under-the-every-student-succeeds-act.

7. For Fryer's account of the Houston program and its results, see Ronald G. Fryer Jr., "Injecting Successful Charter School Strategies into Traditional Public Schools: A Field Experiment in Houston," National Bureau of Economic Research Working Paper No. 17494, October 2011, revised December 2013, http://www.nber.org/papers/w17494. For other accounts of the program and its results, see Margaret Downing, "Apollo 20 Figures Out How to Improve Math Scores, but Reading Remains an Unsolved Equation," *Houston Press*, October 24, 2013, http://www.houstonpress.com/news/apollo-20-figures-out-how-to-improve-math-scores-but-reading-remains-an-unsolved-equation-6744069; Margaret Downing, "Rewriting History: Apollo 20's Legacy as It Is Now, Was Once and What It Was Supposed to Be," *Houston Press*, December 2, 2014, http://www.houstonpress.com/news/rewriting-history-apollo-20s-legacy-as-it-is-now-was-once-and-what-it-was-supposed-to-be-6735683; Amy McCaig, "HISD's Apollo 20 Program Should Expand Tutoring, According to Rice Review," Rice University News and Media, February 12, 2014, http://news.rice.edu/2014/02/12/hisds-apollo-20-program-should-expand-tutoring-according-to-rice-review-2; and Allan Turner, "Review Questions Staying Power of Gains in HISD Apollo Program," *Houston Chronicle*, February 12, 2014, http://www.houstonchronicle.com/houston-texas/houston/article/Review-questions-staying-power-of-gains-in-HISD-5229488.php.

8. Richard P. Phelps, "What the Show-Me Institute Will Not Show Us," *Nonpartisan Education Review/Essays* 14, no. 3 (2018), https://nonpartisaneducation.org/Review/Essays/v14n3.pdf.

9. Richard P. Phelps, "Common Core Collaborators: Six Organizational Portraits," *Nonpartisan Education Review/Articles* 14, no. 3 (2018), https://nonpartisaneducation.org/Review/Articles/CommonCoreCollaborators.htm.

10. Elementary and Secondary Education Act of 1965, H.R. 2362, 89th Cong. (1965), https://www.gpo.gov/fdsys/pkg/STATUTE-79/pdf/STATUTE-79-Pg27.pdf.

11. Williamson M. Evers and Ze'ev Wurman, "California's Common Core Mistake," Defining Ideas, May 9, 2018, https://www.hoover.org/research/californias-common-core-mistake.

12. Evers and Wurman, "California's Common Core Mistake."

13. See, for example, Susan Berry, "Berkeley Math Professor Ratner: Common Core 'Will Move U.S. Closer to Bottom in International Ranking,'" Breitbart, August 6, 2014, https://www.breitbart.com/big-government/2014/08/06/berkeley-math-professor-ratner-common-core-will-move-u-s-closer-to-bottom-in-international-ranking; and Jonathan Goodman, "A Comparison of Common Core Math to Selected Asian Countries," Education News, June 1, 2015, https://www.educationnews.org/education-policy-and-politics/a-comparison-of-common-core-math-to-selected-asian-countries.

14. Evers and Wurman, "California's Common Core Mistake."

15. Staff, "No Intermediate Algebra? No Problem as CSU Ditches Requirement for Non-science, Math Majors in 2018," *Orange County Register*, August 2, 2017, https://www.ocregister.com/2017/08/02/no-intermediate-algebra-no-problem-as-csu-ditches-requirement-for-non-science-math-majors-in-2018; Mikhail Zinshteyn, "Cal State Drops Intermediate Algebra as Requirement to Take Some College-Level Math Courses," EdSource, August 2, 2017, https://edsource.org/2017/cal-state-drops-intermediate-algebra-requirement-allows-other-math-courses/585595.

16. *Massachusetts Curriculum Framework: English Language Arts*, Massachusetts Department of Elementary and Secondary Education, February 1997, http://www.doe.mass.edu/frameworks/ela/1997/strand1.html.

17. Diane Ravitch, "Sandra Stotsky: Massachusetts Excelled without Annual Testing," Education News, January 28, 2016, http://www.educationviews.org/sandra-stotsky-massachusetts-excelled-annual-testing.

18. Sandra Stotsky, "Common Core Doesn't Add Up to STEM Success," *Wall Street Journal*, January 2, 2014, http://www.uaedreform.org/downloads/2014/01/common-core-doesnt-add-up-to-stem-success.pdf.

19. "TIMSS Results Place Massachusetts among World Leaders in Math and Science," press release, Massachusetts Department of Elementary and Secondary Education, December 8, 2008, http://www.doe.mass.edu/news/news.aspx?id=4457.

20. Paul R. Gross, with Douglas Buttrey, Ursula Goodenough, Noretta Koertge, Lawrence Lerner, Martha Schwartz, and Richard Schwartz, *Final Evaluation of the Next Generation Science Standards* (Washington, DC: Thomas B. Fordham Institute, June 2013), https://edexcellence.net/publications/final-evaluation-of-NGSS.html.

21. Personal conversation, 2010.

22. Amazon, "Why Knowledge Matters: Rescuing Our Children from Failed Educational Theories," 2019, https://www.amazon.com/Why-Knowledge-Matters-Rescuing-Educational/dp/1612509525.

23. Liana Heitlin, "*Cultural Literacy* Creator Carries on Campaign," *Education Week*, October 11, 2016, https://www.edweek.org/ew/articles/2016/10/12/cultural-literacy-creator-carries-on-campaign.html.

Chapter Eight

Public Deception

The public has been regularly misled on many issues by policy makers' stated intentions (e.g., "you can keep your doctor"), but perhaps the public has been most misled by their intentions for public education. State boards of education and other policy-making organizations were told that the use of Common Core's English language arts (ELA) standards (and aligned tests) would make all students college- and career-ready. That, of course, has not happened after most states adopted its ELA standards in 2010 or 2011, but the fact that most students are not graduating from high school college-ready or career-ready hasn't diminished policy makers' faith in the effectiveness of these standards. This chapter details some of the ways in which the public has been misled about the efficacy of the standards, their aligned tests, and seemingly revised versions for the states' individual four-year "state plans."

Many years ago, a major goal of education policy makers and researchers was to strengthen the education of low achievers or the children of low-income parents (they weren't necessarily the same children, but they were interchangeable in most policy makers' minds). The best example of that goal is the purpose of the original Elementary and Secondary Education Act (ESEA), passed by Congress in 1965 as part of President Lyndon B. Johnson's War on Poverty: "to strengthen and improve educational quality and educational opportunities in the Nation's elementary and secondary schools."[1]

Indeed, strengthening public education for all was the philosophical goal behind education legislation in California and Massachusetts through the 1990s.[2] It was an accepted fact that, after World War II, the entire sweep of K–12 American education, especially in mathematics, science, and foreign languages, needed to be strengthened. However, the word *strengthen* quickly disappeared in ESEA reauthorization language. It can no longer be found in current Department of Education policies.

Gradually, closing gaps between academically lower and higher achievers became an educational commandment. The implication was that the academic profiles of all politically determined demographic groups should be similar. In 2011, the National Assessment of Educational Progress (NAEP) even put out a chart showing how gaps could be closed hypothetically. In the chart, educators got higher-achieving groups to plateau or decline and lower-achieving groups to learn faster than all others.[3] Not surprisingly, the chart gave no real-world examples.

The 2015 reauthorization of ESEA made it clear that the purpose of the act is "to reauthorize the Elementary and Secondary Education Act of 1965 to ensure that every child achieves."[4] The purpose of Title I is "to provide all children significant opportunity to receive a fair, equitable, and high-quality education, and to close educational achievement gaps."[5] Despite the fact that the education of *all* K–12 students is now governed by federal policies, the title of Title I says only "Improving Basic Programs Operated by State and Local Educational Agencies."[6] There is no mention about the policies having to come from the federal government. How gaps are to be closed by teachers of "basic" programs (whatever that designates) or even by the schools remains a mystery. Many trick-or-treat games have been sold to educators and legislators eager to obtain federal or state money, but educators get the treat (federal or state money) only after someone has played the trick—on the general public. The following are some of the tricks.

HIGHER GRADES FOR THE SAME WORK AND INFLATED (DISHONEST) COURSE TITLES

Grade inflation in high school is common, and it has increased considerably in recent decades. The long-term problem with grade inflation is that many high school students with seemingly high grades enroll in college (or are designated by a test as college-ready) but are vastly unprepared for college-level work.[7] More students than ever today go to college (and are encouraged to do so), but more students than ever are unprepared for college. The evidence: SAT scores have been trending downward nationally since 2004.[8]

That may be why the National Assessment Governing Board (NAGB) is trying to change the cut-off scores for the achievement levels on NAEP tests. No doubt, it wants more students to get scores showing improvement. (NAGB determines NAEP policies.) Recently changed SAT tests have been aligned down to Common Core's high school level, so there will be few differences between the "college-readiness" cut-off score for high school achievement tests (based on Common Core's standards) and the scores on

SAT tests—which were intended to predict success in college.[9] The public was told that aligning SAT tests down to Common Core's college-readiness level would check grade inflation, but there has been no explanation for why aligning SAT tests (and passing scores) with Common Core's college-readiness level would reduce or eliminate grade and course-title inflation.

The real reason for aligning SAT tests down to the college-readiness level for Common Core's high school test may be a defensive one. The public might wonder what a college-readiness level really is if SAT scores show a large number of college-ready students but are contradicted by Common Core–aligned test scores showing these same students are *not* ready for college at all. By aligning SAT scores down to Common Core's high-school-level cut-off for college readiness, SAT officials and Common Core supporters hope to erase any discrepancy between the two tests about who is ready for college or will be successful in college.

Moreover, the Department of Education is taking no chances; it is now allowing states to use the SAT tests in place of a college-readiness test in high school. After all, why should it matter whether a college judges a student to be college-ready based on an SAT test aligned with Common Core or on a college-readiness test based directly on Common Core's standards.

But if all tests are aligned directly or indirectly to tests based on Common Core's standards, why should parents or colleges trust any of them? Parents, states, and researchers once could use college-readiness tests that were independent of Common Core's standards. They can't do that now unless state legislatures pay for all students to participate in international tests, which for now are independent of Common Core (PIRLS and TIMSS).

BIASED SOURCES OF INFORMATION
TO MISLEAD THE PUBLIC

In addition to dishonest grades and course titles, the past decade has witnessed a remarkable number of new organizations and sources of information on education issues and materials.[10] Many seem to be funded, at least in part, by the Gates Foundation, its friends, or both, making them potential outlets for skewed information or talking points. Many, like EdReport and EdSurge, seem to be staffed by young people with little experience in the schools and few, if any, publications in major academic journals. These organizations may retain some editorial independence, but older sources of information (e.g., *Education Week*) may have lost some of their independence when they accepted Gates's subsidies, making it difficult for naïve readers to fully understand a situation or for skeptics to find all the relevant information.

The net result in this expansion of sources (online and in bibliographies) is that it is difficult to trust the information one finds anywhere.[11] Casual readers may not be given all the relevant facts on a particular situation or issue. They may be given only the reasons (from a funder of the source) to support or oppose a particular policy or program. Or the "informational" article may simply be a trial balloon—to find out the position of those who reply quickly.

Before I present an example of deliberate deception—this time in a list of references put out by a college "task force"—readers need to understand that part of the Race to the Top (RttT) project was a concerted effort to eliminate placement tests and developmental courses in mathematics and reading in order to accelerate the college-graduation rate for lower achievers. To facilitate that goal, RttT applications (designed by Joanne Weiss, the chief of staff under Arne Duncan at the Department of Education) asked states (among other things) to commit to the elimination of placement tests, college-level remedial courses (for which no academic credit was usually given), or both and to provide a sign-off from officials at state institutions of higher learning.

Sign-offs came readily, possibly because few public-college presidents wanted to risk a reduction in state appropriations to their institutions if they didn't go along with a new policy for getting more high school graduates declared college-ready (via use of Common Core–aligned tests in high school) and into college. Sign-offs also tended to come from college administrators, not academic deans, possibly because the colleges didn't want to look as if they were bypassing their teaching faculty, who may well have been opposed to eliminating all placement tests for developmental or remedial courses.

In Massachusetts, for example, only a few state college mathematics instructors were asked to participate on a large higher-education task force charged with evaluating developmental courses and placement tests in mathematics at both community and state colleges. Because of minimal participation by relevant faculty, the task force did not hear explanations of why such courses and tests may be useful to the students who take them, one of several problems about this meeting.

In an article published after the Massachusetts Board of Higher Education voted in the policy recommended by the task force, state college faculty in mathematics presented their issues. They could not locate the minutes of the task force's meetings, and they were unable to explain at the board meeting that the references in the task force report were misleading.[12] None of the studies in the report's bibliography provided evidence supporting the task force's recommendations for state colleges: for example, that incoming students benefit from taking mathematics courses beyond their skill level. Indeed, few studies in the annotated references were even relevant to state colleges. The bibliography was skewed toward community colleges, and the information it presented was consistently against the use of placement tests.

In other words, it was a biased bibliography designed to validate a recommendation that had no authentic support.

MISSING RESEARCH

Social promotion is another issue of concern in many schools. Several states have decided to hold back, or retain, grade 3 students who haven't learned to read well enough for grade 4 schoolwork. Peculiarly, in studies of whether retention is useful, researchers and staff at state departments of education do not usually investigate how the retained students were taught to read in kindergarten, grade 1, and grade 2 or how their teachers were taught to teach beginning reading in their preparation or professional-development programs.[13] Instead, they look at the grade 3 reading program (classroom libraries, books for preschoolers, literacy coaches, an early-reading curriculum, and an extended day, as in Muskegon, Michigan) or at the results of retention after students have moved to a higher grade, as in Florida, Michigan, and North Carolina.[14] The public is misled into thinking that their public schools are finally looking into the problem of social promotion and getting relevant evidence.

In many (if not all) cases, however, little has been learned about why these children cannot read by grade 3. The conclusion of this incomplete research is usually that retention doesn't seem to be a useful policy and that social promotion should continue. But in reality, beginning reading may not be taught appropriately in the primary grades or in teacher training, and a school board should first find out why kids have not learned to read by grade 3 before voting for or against a social-promotion policy—that is, *if* educators want to find out whether some roots of reading failure are in their own schools.

DISTORTED RESEARCH FINDINGS

The subheadline of a 2016 article in the *Atlantic* shouts, "Half a century ago, the Coleman Report revealed that socioeconomic diversity is key to removing racial inequalities in education."[15] The chief problem with this is that it is *not* what the Coleman report revealed. It found, as earlier chapters point out, that a child's academic achievement is better explained by the family's background than by the child's teachers or schools. That doesn't make socioeconomic diversity the key. If anything, it makes the child's family the key. But by omitting what the Coleman report actually found, we avoid a discussion of possible policies that could directly address the roots of racial group inequalities in education.

That subheadline does not make magnet schools the solution to integration, regardless of how useful such schools may be in providing families with alternative choices in a school district. (The article promotes magnet schools.) Integration of differently populated school districts is one way to address the Coleman report finding that the peer environment in a low-performing school may be one cause of low student achievement. But although some studies have shown positive effects on student achievement from socioeconomic integration of school populations, it did not have the same effects everywhere.[16] An August 2016 Brookings Institution article concludes that it is not at all clear that the social and educational benefits of integration outweigh the costs.[17]

James Coleman himself seemed to have little problem with desegregation in the form of court-mandated busing schemes until they led to "white flight." At that point, he made it clear that such schemes work only so long as most of the children in the school being integrated were white. This led some black parents to complain that integration meant that their youngsters couldn't learn unless most of their classmates were white—a rather insulting insinuation—and that black students had to chase white populations wherever they moved. However, integration is no longer a major goal of education policy. Closing gaps is, although one wonders why it is also not insulting when African Americans are at the bottom of every education index that the Department of Education puts out just because it wants to highlight differences in academic achievement that teachers should focus on. It must be depressing for black students to see themselves regularly placed in the lowest education categories that media and education researchers publish.

WITHHOLDING RELEVANT INFORMATION FROM PARENTS

After Every Student Succeeds Act (ESSA) was passed by Congress in December 2015 as a reauthorization of the 1965 Elementary and Secondary Education Act, Senator Lamar Alexander, a cosponsor of the bill, claimed it returned some authority back to the states and local governments. To date, parents have not been able to find any authority returned to local control, including the consequences for opt-outs, which are constitutionally under local school boards, not state boards or the Department of Education.

Indeed, Peter Cunningham, former assistant secretary for communications at the Department of Education under Secretary of Education Arne Duncan, labeled Senator Alexander's comment on the passage of Every Student Succeeds Act "misleading." In a blog at the *Education Post*, Cunningham notes that Senator Alexander claimed that he ran for reelection on a promise to "repeal the federal Common Core mandate and reverse the trend toward a national school board."[18] Cunningham then snarls,

> There never was a Common Core mandate so the new law can't repeal what didn't exist. There was an incentive to adopt "college- and career-ready" standards in the . . . Race to the Top grant program. But it wasn't a mandate. It was voluntary. Moreover, under the new law [i.e., ESSA], every state must adopt "college- and career-ready" standards. Thus, the new law all but guarantees that Common Core State Standards—or a reasonable imitation under a different name—will likely remain in place in most states. [19]

In other words, parents were misinformed by a sponsor of the bill about what the bill did. Moreover, Cunningham's remarks make it clear that "college- and career-ready" standards are basically Common Core standards, even if those words are not used.

ESSA also requires all details in the four-year state plan to be reviewed and approved by the Department of Education. The plan must contain the details for a report card that the federal government wants all states to use, which is so complex that the Department of Education has prepared a guide to help parents understand what is on their children's report card.[20] Surely, Senator Alexander understands that federal or state control of a local school's report card means no local control.

NON-EVIDENCE-BASED HIGH SCHOOL DIPLOMAS FOR SKILLS-BASED LEARNING

Some education "reformers" are trying to change what high school diplomas are awarded for—often in the name of preparing students for a global twenty-first-century economy (meaning no more valedictorians, salutatorians, class ranks, honor rolls, top 10 percent, sports eligibility, etc.). The Maine legislature voted in 2012 for proficiency-based diplomas for the state. The Nellie Mae Foundation based in Massachusetts decided to help Maine educators to get rid of "traditional" markers for academic achievement in favor of ways to reward "what students can do," not what they know. Their consultants traveled the state to persuade superintendents and school boards to adopt what a parent in York, Maine, refers to as an "untested and unproven method of teaching, learning, and grading."[21]

Because Maine was the first state in the nation to require a proficiency-based high school diploma, it is useful for other states to find out what happened in Maine: enormous pushback by teachers and parents and, ultimately, a reversal in 2018 of the legislature's mandate for skills-based high school diplomas![22] According to the new legislation, it is now a Maine school district's choice whether to award students a "traditional" high school diploma or a competency-based diploma. It was a brilliant compromise. Not only did it give some teeth back to those advocating local control, but it also gave educators promoting skills-based diplomas time to develop support in their local communities for the new idea and find evidence that competency-based (skills-based) diplomas are worth the effort and expense to do over the entire public educational system.

We need to notice the reasons given for what happened in Maine. Nellie Mae and others agreed that "personalized" learning capped by a competency-based diploma had been poorly implemented, an excuse similar to the one that had been offered when many teachers and parents protested the standards funded by the Gates Foundation and adopted by their states' boards of education in 2010 and 2011. Moreover, there was little evidence of the benefits of skills-based diplomas and no evidence in Maine or elsewhere that recent changes in the educational system helped low-achieving students from low-income families to learn even as much as before and to develop critical-thinking skills.

The chaos in the schools conveyed by all the reporters who report on teachers' and parents' criticisms overwhelms a reader. Vermont towns are divided about skills-based diplomas.[23] New Hampshire decided on a slower pace years ago, allowing about twenty years for school districts to move from diploma credits based on "seat-time" to credits based on mastery of competencies or skills, "as in personalized learning."[24] It is unclear if New Hampshire high schools will still give academic credit to mastery based on knowledge about a subject. It is clear that the term *seat-time* is being used rhetorically by state officials to avoid admitting that the real counterpart to skills or competencies is academic coursework or knowledge-based courses.

In his article on Maine, *Chalkbeat* reporter Matt Barnum comments, "Forty-eight states have adopted policies to promote 'competency-based' education to varying degrees, often at the urging of a constellation of influential philanthropies, including the Nellie Mae Foundation, which poured at least $13 million into Maine's effort."[25] To date, it seems, no state has finished redoing an education system crowned by competency-based diplomas, and no state-level school officials in Maine, Vermont, and New Hampshire are quoted as wondering what the major problems implementing such a system might be. As Barnum further notes, "There remains little evidence that proficiency-based education has boosted student learning, in Maine or elsewhere."[26] One wonders why parents and teachers weren't told this to begin with and why a state legislature passed a law promoting it in the absence of evidence for its benefits.

EXCLUSION OF ACADEMIC EXPERTS
IN JUDGING COLLEGE READINESS

The public was deceived nationwide when the language in ESSA made it clear that local school boards can do little, if anything, to respond to classroom-based concerns even though Senator Lamar Alexander of Tennessee, a cosponsor of the 2015 reauthorization of ESEA, claimed that ESSA was intended to reduce federal authority over local education, or federal overreach. ESSA's goal is not to strengthen public education but to "close gaps"—two very different directions for a K–12 curriculum. And apparently the only way gaps can be closed is by centralizing educational policy making in a distant federal bureaucracy so that it can't be altered by local educators (teachers and administrators); parents; and citizens across the range of professions, organizations, and businesses that dominate local and state political life—all while they are told that federal authority is being reduced and skills are being taught.

That seems to be the basic purpose of the four-year "state plans" submitted in 2016 by state departments of education wanting Title I money. As anticipated, most, if not all, states wanted money. Opting children out of state-required tests is penalized by state authorities, even though constitutionally the consequences of parents exercising this right are to be decided by local boards of education.

The plan itself had to be formulated and submitted by a state department of education, with or without a governor's signature, for review and approval by the US Department of Education. No reviews and approval from a state legislature, local parent organizations, *or* state or local teacher or administrator professional organizations were needed. Such reviews were not expressly forbidden, but they were not mentioned as necessary for submission of a four-year state plan to the Department of Education. The federal government calls all the shots directly or through its fifty satellites—state departments of education or public instruction and probably their commissioners and superintendents of education.

That may be why state departments of education deliberately failed to ask for the judgment of real experts in English language arts and mathematics at their own public colleges and universities when adopting the K–12 standards in 2016 for the state plans. Not one state board or department of education asked for or got advice from a group of experts in the humanities, engineering, science, or mathematics on whether the high school standards in English, mathematics, and (later) science under consideration would (when teachers taught to them) help to make the state's high school students college-ready. An analysis of the "revised" standards by teaching faculty in introductory college courses was not wanted, and yet, they were the only ones who could judge college readiness.

Elected and appointed public officials again deceived parents. The standards that state boards adopted in 2010 and 2011 were approved mostly by state boards incapable of evaluating high school standards in mathematics and English. At that time, too, these boards tended to rely on recommendations from nonexpert staff in their own departments of education and their commissioners of education or on the testimony from members of the three agencies funded by the Bill and Melinda Gates Foundation to corroborate each other: Council for Chief State School Officers (CCSSO); National Governors Association (NGA); and Achieve, Inc., an organization established earlier by the NGA.

At their first adoption of skills-based standards in 2010 and 2011, state boards generally knew nothing about the lack of qualifications of the lead writers chosen to write them. Its members did not engage in the kind of inquiry they likely would have undertaken individually when choosing a surgeon for a needed medical operation. The organizations that developed these standards have never told the public who recommended these people as standards writers, why, and how much were they paid. From their affiliations, we know that the main advisory groups helping to write Common Core's standards consisted chiefly of test and curriculum developers from ACT, College Board, Achieve, and National Center on Education and the Economy (NCEE).

We also know that the two large work groups also helping the writers did not include current high school English and mathematics teachers, English professors, scientists, engineers, parents, state legislators, early childhood educators, and state or local school board members.[27] The work groups held no open meetings and have never provided access to any public comment or critiques they received.

Professional organizations with expertise in English or reading have not evaluated the quality of Common Core's ELA standards (e.g., National Council of Teachers of English, International Reading Association, Modern Language Association), no matter what name a state has given their slightly revised version of them. Nor have professional organizations with expertise in mathematics (e.g., American Mathematical Society) evaluated its math standards.[28] Not one reporter, to our knowledge, has ever wondered why—in public. It remains an amazing phenomenon.

The media has not shown the slightest interest in the *qualifications* of the standards writers or commented on the *low level* of college readiness they determined. If they had sought information on the qualifications of the lead writers for Common Core's ELA standards, they would have found that David Coleman and Susan Pimentel had never taught reading or English in K–12 or at the college level. Neither had majored in English as undergraduates or had a doctorate in English. Neither had published serious work on K–12 curriculum and instruction. At the time, they were unknown to English and reading educators and to higher-education faculty in rhetoric, speech, composition, and literary study. The third member of this standards-writing team, James Patterson, held a position at a testing company. His role in the team's work is unclear.

Two of the lead standards writers in mathematics did have academic credentials—they knew what topics should be studied in advanced high school mathematics and science courses—but no K–12 teaching experience. Nor had either ever developed K–12 mathematics standards before. Jason Zimba was a physics professor at Bennington College at the time, while William McCallum was (and remains) a mathematics professor at the University of Arizona. The only member of this three-person team with K–12 teaching experience, Phil Daro, had majored in English as an undergraduate; he was also on the staff of the NCEE, headed by Marc Tucker. And together they ensured that Common Core's math standards went only as high as Algebra II "lite" for college readiness but no further.

SUMMARY

Although postsecondary degrees from two- and three-year community colleges and four-year state colleges may now be perceived as fairer "sorting" devices than GEDs or high school diplomas, it is not clear to education policy makers how to prepare any students in public high schools for authentic college work. Common Core's standards apply to students in public charter high schools and public high schools, so they reach most students in this country. However, they do not reach academically beyond grade 8 or 9 in English, mathematics, and science.

It now appears that the Department of Education has a major dilemma: how to structure authentic preparation for college work between early adolescence (in middle schools and junior high schools) and late adolescence (in community or state colleges) and then how to choose the students for this new structure. High schools may soon be declared obsolete. The reading level of most high school textbooks and literary texts is already at about grade 7 or 8, but a huge gap remains between what is being taught in middle schools and junior high schools and what is expected of freshmen in authentic undergraduate coursework in liberal arts and engineering colleges here or in other countries.

KEY IDEAS TO REMEMBER

1. The public has been misled in many ways on the intentions of education policy makers in the past half-century.

2. After World War II, there was a national consensus that public education needed to be strengthened. Instead, after the passage of the Elementary and Secondary Education Act in 1965, Congress changed its focus and has regularly appropriated funds for K–12 education to improve the academic status of low achievers, not strengthen their schools or teachers.

3. Congress has been highly unsuccessful in its new focus but does not learn from its failures. In fact, its failures seem to drive federal policy makers in education (at the Department of Education) to greater and greater efforts to nationalize all education policies in the name of closing academic gaps between low-achieving demographic groups and higher-achieving white students, even though one small minority group (Asian Americans) scores higher on average than all other groups and continues annually to widen the gaps between their academic performance and that of all other groups.

4. To rationalize what they do, education policy makers at all levels of government, backed by the philanthropists and organizations supporting them, deceive parents and other citizens in a variety of ways.

5. Among the ways in which education policy makers or others may deceive the public are (1) inflating course grades and titles in K–12 to provide dishonest information, (2) providing biased sources of information on talking points, (3) avoiding observational research on beginning reading pedagogy in teachers' classrooms or training programs, (4) distorting the findings of studies that are incompatible with the narrative being promoted, (5) withholding relevant information, (6) changing high school graduation requirements from coursework in knowledge and critical thinking to ungraded, content-less skills, and (7) excluding academic experts from serving as judges of college readiness.

NOTES

1. Elementary and Secondary Education Act of 1965, H.R. 2362, 89th Cong. (1965), https://www.gpo.gov/fdsys/pkg/STATUTE-79/pdf/STATUTE-79-Pg27.pdf.

2. See, for example, the Massachusetts Education Reform Act of 1993; and Assembly Bill No. 265 (Chapter 975, Statutes of 1995), the Leroy Greene California Assessment of Academic Achievement Act, http://leginfo.ca.gov/pub/95-96/bill/asm/ab_0251-0300/ab_265_bill_951016_chaptered.pdf.

3. "Understanding Gaps," National Assessment of Educational Progress, National Center for Education Statistics, https://nces.ed.gov/nationsreportcard/studies/gaps/understand_gaps.aspx.

4. Every Student Succeeds Act of 2015, PL 114–95 129 Stat. 1814 (December 10, 2015), https://congress.gov/114/plaws/publ95/PLAW-114publ95.pdf.

5. Every Student Succeeds Act of 2015, PL 114–95 129 Stat. 1814 (December 10, 2015), https://congress.gov/114/plaws/publ95/PLAW-114publ95.pdf.

6. Every Student Succeeds Act of 2015, PL 114–95 129 Stat. 1814 (December 10, 2015), https://congress.gov/114/plaws/publ95/PLAW-114publ95.pdf.

7. Samantha Lindsay, "Is Grade Inflation in High School Real?" *PrepScholar* (blog), November 4, 2018, https://blog.prepscholar.com/grade-inflation-high-school.

8. Alexandra Pannoni, "3 Answers for Parents about High School Grade Inflation," *US News and World Report*, July 31, 2017, https://www.yahoo.com/news/3-answers-parents-high-school-grade-inflation-120000928.html.

9. Stuart Seputro, "What Is the Purpose of SAT?" *Quora*, May 19, 2018, https://www.quora.com/What-is-the-purpose-of-SAT.

10. See, for example, "Our Mission," EdReports, https://www.edreports.org/about/index.html.

11. Karen R. Effrem, "Flawed Report Uses Pseudoscience to Promote 'Social Emotional Learning,'" *National Pulse*, October 17, 2018, https://thenationalpulse.com/commentary/flawed-report-uses-pseudoscience-promote-social-emotional-learning.

12. Mike Winders and Richard Bisk, "Math Task Force's Bad Calculation," *New England Journal of Higher Education*, September 30, 2014, https://nebhe.org/journal/math-task-forces-bad-calculation/.

13. See, for example, Jennifer Palmer, "Oklahoma Near Top in Holding Back Young Students," *Enid News and Eagle*, December 17, 2018, https://www.enidnews.com/news/state/oklahoma-near-top-in-holding-back-young-students/article_b0ab0c6f-4177-54ff-844a-4bb46b6946f0.html.

14. Ron French, "Muskegon Kids Struggle to Read. Their Superintendent Had the Same Problem," Bridge, September 17, 2018, https://www.bridgemi.com/talent-education/muskegon-kids-struggle-read-their-superintendent-had-same-problem; Ann Doss Helms, "Why Can't NC Kids Read? Another Study Shows Read to Achieve Produced No Gains," *Charlotte Observer*, October 22, 2018, https://www.charlotteobserver.com/news/local/education/article220318855.html.

15. Richard D. Kahlenberg, "Why Did It Take So Long for Class-Based School Integration to Take Hold?" *Atlantic*, July 2, 2016, https://www.theatlantic.com/education/archive/2016/07/why-did-it-take-so-long-for-class-based-school-integration-to-take-hold/489863.

16. Susan Eaton and Steven Rivkin, "Is Desegregation Dead?" *EducationNext* 10, no. 4 (Fall 2010): 50–59, http://educationnext.org/is-desegregation-dead.

17. David Armor, "Bringing Back Busing: Do Benefits Outweigh Cost?" *Brown Center Chalkboard* (blog), August 23, 2016, https://www.brookings.edu/blog/brown-center-chalkboard/2016/08/23/bringing-back-busing-do-benefits-outweigh-cost.

18. Lamar Alexander, "Law Ends Common Core Mandate, Strengthens Local Control," *Tennessean*, December 12, 2015, https://www.tennessean.com/story/opinion/contributors/2015/12/11/law-ends-common-core-mandate-strengthens-local-control/77117180/; Peter Cunningham, "Senator Alexander's Misleading Victory Lap," Education Post, December 13, 2015, https://educationpost.org/senator-alexanders-misleading-victory-lap/.

19. Cunningham, "Senator Alexander's Victory Lap."

20. Susan Berry, "DeVos Releases 'Guide' for Parents to Understand Report Cards Mandated by Federal Law," Education News, November 9, 2018, www.educationviews.org/devos-releases-guide-for-parents-to-understand-report-cards-mandated-by-federal-law.

21. Julie Edminster, "Proficiency-Based Grading Hurts College Admissions," Seacoastonline.com, April 8, 2018, http://www.seacoastonline.com/news/20180408/proficiency-based-grading-hurts-college-admissions.

22. Matt Barnum, "Maine Went All In on 'Proficiency-Based Learning'—Then Rolled It Back. What Does That Mean for the Rest of the Country?" Chalkbeat, October 18, 2018, https://chalkbeat.org/posts/us/2018/10/18/maine-went-all-in-on-proficiency-based-learning-then-rolled-it-back-what-does-that-mean-for-the-rest-of-the-country.

23. Tiffany Danitz Pache, "Communities Divided over Proficiency-Based Testing," VTDigger, April 8, 2018, https://vtdigger.org/2018/04/08/communities-divided-proficiency-based-learning.

24. Dale Frost, "How New Hampshire Transformed to a Competency-Based System," iN-ACOL, May 10, 2016, https://www.inacol.org/news/how-new-hampshire-transformed-to-a-competency-based-system/.

25. Barnum, "Maine Went All In."

26. Barnum, "Maine Went All In."

27. Sandra Stotsky, "Common Core Facts," Pioneer Institute, http://pioneerinstitute.org/wp-content/uploads/Common-Core-Fact-Sheet_new.pdf.

28. The mode of analysis typically undertaken by education researchers and state departments of education is called a "crosswalk," a comparison that tries to match the content in one set of standards to the content in the other by grade level. However, crosswalks have serious deficiencies. They cannot indicate that both sets may be weak (they show only how the possibly weak content in one set of standards matches the weak content in another set). They also do not capture the features of ELA standards that determine their rigor and coherence. For more details, see Sandra Stotsky, "9 Signs of Academic Rigor in English Standards," Pioneer Institute, August 7, 2013, https://pioneerinstitute.org/blog/9-signs-of-academic-rigor-in-english-standards-by-sandra-stotsky/.

Chapter Nine

Gap Closing as an Unworkable Educational Goal

In the famous evacuation from the beaches and harbor of Dunkirk, France, between May 26 and June 4, 1940, about 200,000 soldiers in the British Expeditionary Force were saved, along with thousands of soldiers from allied countries that had already formally surrendered or, in the case of France, were about to surrender to the Germans. Instead of an expected 35,000 soldiers saved, there were about 340,000. Commenting on the "miracle at Dunkirk," Winston Churchill quipped, "We must be very careful not to assign to this deliverance the attributes of a victory. Wars are not won by evacuations."

Nor is public education strengthened by standards, tests, and a K–12 curriculum whose seeming purpose is to equalize the achievement of an expanding variety of student groups across ethnic, racial, and socioeconomic lines. The purpose of the Elementary and Secondary Education Act of 1965 has evolved from strengthening public education and the education of children in low-income families to closing the gaps between demographic groups of those with higher test scores and those with lower test scores to ensure an "equitable" education for all groups. [1]

This chapter points out some of the educational issues in implementing this new goal for public education and some of the new policies being used to implement it. The latest group to be added by the Department of Education to the list of low achievers are children raised in foster homes. [2] Even if academic gaps are closed, most members of these demographics may end up academically weaker than they now are. No one promised that gaps would be closed at a *higher* academic level.

Is a gap-less classroom one in which all students, regardless of politically defined demographic group, learn the same amount, know the same things, and think alike? How does a teacher at any grade and in any subject aim for such a classroom by May or June? Should teachers expect all students to make gains but expect the lowest achievers to make greater gains than the highest achievers? Or should teachers expect only the lowest achievers to make gains while all higher achievers are held back in some way (a phenomenon known as lowering the ceiling)? Should teachers ensure that low achievers decline less than higher achievers? Policy makers can try to convince parents that all students have learned more, based on the theory that less is more, or that they have developed critical-thinking skills, but this is a tough sell—not easy to demonstrate.

State boards of elementary, secondary, and higher education as well as state departments of education have been led to believe that gaps might close if they did the following: (1) Ignore what their own college teaching faculty in English and mathematics would tell them about what high school students need to know or be able to do for college-level work. (2) Use scores on tests of college and career readiness (tests aligned with gap-closing standards, whatever their actual name) rather than scores on unaligned tests (such as the old SAT or ACT or the new Classic Learning Test, or CLT) in grade 11 or 12 to try to ensure higher pass rates for a high school diploma or the status of being college-ready.[3] And (3) ensure that English and reading teachers assign harder, more complex texts to all students using the student's grade level, not reading level, as their guide.[4] Needless to say, gaps would widen, not close, if they subscribed fully to those three articles of faith. But many educators today prefer to believe in a Tooth Fairy.

HOW TEACHERS TRY TO CLOSE GAPS

So far, the Department of Education has issued no guidelines to classroom teachers on exactly how to close gaps. It has ensured, by means of the approval process required in Every Student Succeeds Act (ESSA), that all state plans commit to the use of gap-closing standards (a.k.a., college- and career-ready standards) and state tests aligned to them. But we don't know from the Department of Education how teachers of any subject are to organize learning activities that close gaps or could close gaps under the right conditions (e.g., if more money is allocated by the district, state, or federal government for this goal).

In the absence of specific classroom-level guidelines from the Department of Education and state departments of education, teachers will try to close gaps the only way they know how: follow what they are told to do with the curriculum materials given them, all of which tend to include less content, although they are not described that way. The materials may have activities for addressing social and emotional learning (SEL) standards but not indicate that academic content has been reduced to make room for SEL activities. All that teachers and parents may be told is what has been added. Common sense alone suggests that, if something has been added, then something must have been subtracted, unless the school day was lengthened. What has been subtracted is usually not indicated, and few if any teachers or parents ask.

Teach Less Content

Presently, "deeper learning" is a frequent goal used by curriculum supervisors to justify teaching less content. Tom Loveless, an education researcher, describes it as a strategy for organizing content in a K–12 curriculum leading to less discipline-based content learning:

> Deeper learning, like its intellectual ancestors [project-based learning, inquiry and discovery learning, higher-level thinking, critical thinking, outcome-based education, and twenty-first-century skills], tries to . . . upend the pre-eminence of knowledge. These ideas . . . share one characteristic. All are advertised as . . . superior to academic content organized within traditional intellectual disciplines.[5]

Many teachers probably do not view what they do today as teaching less, which results in students learning less, as in the arithmetic example that Loveless discusses. Teachers are usually not told what content has been removed from earlier sets of grade-level standards. Nor have they been given any evidence that all students learn something at a deeper level of understanding when they are asked to write an explanation and sometimes to draw pictures of an acceptable thinking process behind the basic arithmetic operation they have been asked to perform on a test. Describing their thinking process on an arithmetic test does *not* mean that deeper learning has taken place for students, but it could mean that students have *not* been taught to use or have simply been forbidden to show use of the relevant standard algorithm for performing an arithmetic operation. Teachers have not been told why grade 8 and high school National Assessment of Educational Progress (NAEP) mathematics test scores don't show increases in student achievement after a half-dozen or more years of lessons and activities leading to deeper learning.

However, future tests may well show that there has been student progress in mathematics (and science) once the present cut-off scores for performance levels are lowered. This is something the National Assessment Governing Board (NAGB), in charge of NAEP test policies, may be hoping to accomplish in the near future.[6] But a lower cut-off score for a performance level may *not* mean that it was originally set too high but that the cut-off score had to be lowered to make it look as if more students had improved over time. An independent analysis is needed to determine whether students made real progress in ELA (e.g., by looking at writing samples).

What might teachers do to teach less content? In lessons on this country's seminal political documents, reading or English teachers may teach less simply by engaging their students in experience-based discussions on a current event or historical speech, mainly because these teachers were not history majors and cannot provide much, *if any*, historical context for the event or speech.[7] As another example, teachers may give a history lesson in the form of an in-class writing exercise, as suggested by an online lesson for "literacy" teaching.[8] They may tell students exactly what texts to read and what questions to answer, even in grade 8, because, it is implied, students do not know how to write up their own ideas, and equity requires equal learning opportunities, even if these learning opportunities assume they all know very little. Moreover, when excessive time is spent on in-class writing, time on teaching content through whole-class discussions is reduced.

Gap closing as an educational goal has had damaging effects on teachers as much as on their students. It cloaks in deceptive language strategies for lowering the ceiling and makes inexperienced teachers think that pedagogical activities promoted in the name of gap closing actually help all students to learn more or think better. But it offers no proof that it does! In fact, this country has little to show for the half-dozen years in which most states have used the gap-closing standards adopted in 2010 or 2011. Instead, academic differences between low and high achievers have been widening nationally on NAEP tests.

In Massachusetts, the 2015 tests aligned to gap-closing standards were deceptively labeled MCAS 2.0, or Next-Generation MCAS, because of earlier, state-developed tests called the Massachusetts Comprehensive Assessment System.[9] The new tests used the original name because they were to be given in Massachusetts, but unlike the original MCAS tests, they are *not* based on the state's pre–Common Core standards.

In 2017, Rhode Island's department of education arranged to use some of the Bay State's current MCAS 2.0 tests, but officials in Rhode Island didn't seem to understand that they were not getting tests based on first-rate standards. The end result: Rhode Island gave tests aligned to the same gap-closing standards that the Bay State currently uses *and* that Rhode Island had been using prior to the arrangement.[10]

Although scores for two low-achieving groups have declined in recent years in the Bay State,[11] a Massachusetts-based organization called FairTest has regularly expressed concerns about using "standardized" tests like MCAS 2.0 to assess *student understanding* of a state's gap-closing standards. FairTest expresses little concern about the *standards* themselves. In place of standardized tests, FairTest wants "performance assessments," which are expensive and unreliable.

Not only have national education policy makers expressed few concerns about the widening gaps (between high and low achievers) on NAEP tests despite gap-closing standards and the tests based on them, but there have also been no protests by minority parents or others in the Bay State about the decline in minority group scores since the implementation of its new (gap-closing) standards and tests. If anything, educators and administrators complain about not having enough money to implement the new standards, but claiming that more money is needed makes the public think that teachers are the basic problem, not the standards they must teach.

For example, despite having the highest test opt-out rate of K–12 students in the country, the New York State Board of Regents in 2017 approved *Next-Generation Learning Standards* after the state's department of education only slightly revised the original Common Core–based standards. No matter how they are described, the revised standards are heavy on technology use and require endless teacher professional development, and they will not make all students any more college-ready than Common Core did.

The appeal of gap closing in 2010 is difficult to understand—unless state departments of education felt deeply guilty about something they had not done or did not understand themselves. More than forty-five state boards of education in 2010 and 2011 agreed to adopt gap-closing standards, despite their lack of understanding of the content for an academic high school curriculum in mathematics, science, history, and English or the rationale for this content. Moreover, there are no reports of state board members asking to hear from large groups of experienced high school teachers in each subject in their own state—in person or through a survey about the proposed standards.

State boards of education also failed to ask college teaching faculty in science, mathematics, and English to provide the public with independent, anonymous analyses of the high school gap-closing standards under consideration. At least, there are no reports by college teaching faculty who had been invited by their state boards to analyze prospective 9–12 state standards claiming to prepare all students to be college-ready.

Don't Ask College Teaching Faculty
What College Readiness Means

There are several reasons a state board or department of education might not have wanted the advice of the teaching faculty in their state colleges about the high school standards under consideration. It may not have wanted its own higher-education faculty to influence content, even though college faculty teach many of the state's future teachers in their arts and sciences courses, as well as other students, and are apt to have the most informed advice on what college readiness should mean.

Probably the major reason that college teaching faculty were not invited to offer their professional judgments was that state departments of education had been advised to increase the graduation rate of high school students. Students were all to be college-ready once K–12 teachers addressed the new college-ready standards (in more than forty-five states). Boards and governors did not want to upset that applecart and strengthen the K–12 curriculum, making it likely that fewer rather than more students would go on to college.

Some strategizing had already gone into increasing high school graduation rates and college enrollment, as well as college graduation rates. Because this country has one of the highest rates of high school and college graduates in the world, lower achievers in the high school population have been a frequent target of Department of Education strategy: how to get more of them into college. As of the 2015 census, about **88** percent of US adults held a high school diploma or GED, while about 33 percent held a bachelor's degree or higher.[12] But the goal was more college graduates, not better-educated adults *who might be* college graduates.

Policies that many high schools and colleges now use to increase high school graduation rates, college enrollment, and college graduation rates include:

- **Dual Credit:** Some high schools and colleges have adopted a policy called dual credit or dual enrollment. Such a collaborative effort enables an eligible high school student to take a course at a nearby college and simultaneously earn college and high school credit. Is it a good idea? Raymund Paredes, commissioner of higher education in Texas, explains why dual-credit access without adequate academic preparation is not promising for low-income students. The policy in Texas has not necessarily worked well for Texas students, many of whom are Hispanics.[13]
- **Early College High Schools:** Specialized high schools with demanding courses to put students on track to earn an associate degree while in high school have been established and funded to increase the graduation rate of high school students and their enrollment in college. College credit from the colleges partnered with such high schools may be awarded for high school coursework deemed equivalent to college coursework, but conditions vary across high schools. Some colleges may not award their own credit for courses taken in a high school and taught by a high school teacher. It is not clear how many students today have earned both a high school diploma and an associate degree in an early college high school.
- **Elimination of Developmental Courses:** Sometimes state boards of education have ignored their own college-freshmen-teaching faculty in order to increase the graduation rate of the low-achieving students that their own colleges admit. Race to the Top applications required sign-offs from college administrators (not academic teaching faculty) if they agreed to eliminate remedial or developmental courses in their colleges.

- **Corequisites:** Another policy to increase college graduation rates is the use of corequisites. Corequisites are courses that must be taken simultaneously if the student wants credit for both courses. Many of the programs involving corequisites have been effective. [14]

Don't Evaluate Academic Results of Policies to Increase Graduation Rates

Both high schools and colleges have been encouraged by Department of Education policies to prevent dropouts, accelerate student progress toward a diploma, and increase graduation rates. It's unclear if lower achievers graduate from high school as authentically college-ready in the absence of independent tests of academic achievement—tests that have *not* been aligned to states' newly adopted standards. States that registered as separate countries and have students randomly sampled for Trends in International Mathematics and Science Study tests (TIMSS) for grades 4 and 8 *can* find out how their own students compare internationally. The others cannot.

Once a high school diploma meant that a high school graduate could likely read at a high school level. Today, the *average* American college freshman reads at a grade 6 or 7 level. [15] Undergraduate colleges have often been judged by the average SAT or ACT scores of their freshman class, but the alignment of SAT or ACT tests down to the level of states' high school standards makes the meaning of the average SAT or ACT score of the entering freshman class unclear (especially now that high schools have been allowed to substitute the SAT or ACT tests for high school exit tests), and the public doesn't know how exactly the cut-off scores are set for these tests. How lower reading and writing levels have affected the meaning of a college degree or enrollment in some majors or areas of concentration is not clear. And how lower reading and writing levels affect graduate study in such professions as nursing, engineering, or medicine is unknown.

Part of this country's education problem is the unwillingness of policy makers to accept a normal curvelike distribution of academic effort and academic scores after the primary grades (K, 1, and 2). It was once commonly understood that, in a large normal population, a small number of students would be very high achievers, a small number would be very low achievers, but most would be about average or a little above or below. While some students would learn a lot faster than others, most would not. But all would respect school staff and school rules and find school-related activities to absorb their energy. Neither students nor parents years ago saw teachers or school administrators as the cause of a normal-curve spread of general attitudes toward schoolwork—a phenomenon that has long existed.

Improve Students' Self-Esteem

The self-esteem movement that erupted in the 1970s was one of the earliest waves of explanations for low achievement, and it was followed by expensive advice on teacher pedagogy to foster self-esteem.[16] Education school faculty, professional developers, and public lecturers explained to prospective and practicing teachers (and young parents) how to improve self-esteem. It would solve, they claimed, the problem of low achievement.

However, there were many developmental and psychological complexities. Several researchers suggested that, although praise for effort is effective in some respects in early childhood, it often stops working and even backfires by adolescence. The researchers who proposed this idea also explained their findings psychologically. Praise, they claimed, can communicate that effort is a path to improving ability but can also imply that students need to work hard because of low innate ability.[17] So, damned if you do, and damned if you don't!

Not only did the ideas of self-esteem advocates not work, but also they left educational and cultural debris for others to clean up.[18] According to the critics of the original self-esteem movement, parents and teachers had been told to praise children for their intelligence, not their effort. The critics complained that this praise was damaging, mainly because over the long run it made students overconfident, aggressive, and competitive—contrary to what was intended. What all students needed was serious, constructive criticism.

Indeed, that was what teachers were expected to provide years ago, before the self-esteem movement, which raises the questions, Why did most educators subscribe to the new ideas on self-esteem sweeping the country in the 1980s? Why did obvious fads costing a lot of taxpayer money take possession of otherwise normal, cautious, even skeptical people (most teachers and administrators)? Parents might also want to know why this educational fad was so appealing when there was no evidence of its effectiveness. But, as Yogi Berra is reported as saying, it was déjà vu all over again.

An extension of the self-esteem movement is the advice teachers are now getting about the difficulty level of the texts they assign in an English or reading class. The latest twist is that teachers should use the student's grade level, not reading level, to guide their choice of book for class discussion or study. This means that, if a fifth-grader can read at a high school level, then the teacher may be advised to assign books with a fifth-grade reading level to the child. Conversely, if a high school student reads at a fifth-grade level, then the teacher may be advised to assign that student books at a high school level (i.e., far beyond the student's ability). The idea is that all students at any particular grade should be reading at that grade level in English or reading so that no one's self-esteem is inflated or deflated, regardless if struggling readers have the vocabulary to comprehend what they are reading or faster learners are bored.

A 2018 report issued by Fordham Institute strongly advises using students' grade level, not reading level. Based on a large sample of teachers, the report found that, "five years after implementation of the Common Core State Standards in reading," more teachers are choosing texts based on students' reading level instead of their grade level—even though the Fordham Institute acknowledges that the standards encourage the opposite.[19] According to the study, between 2012 and 2017, the percentage of teachers who said they were more likely to choose texts based on students' grade level decreased from 38 percent to 26 percent. Conversely, the percentage who said they were more likely to base their choices on students' reading level increased from 39 percent to 57 percent. An outside observer might conclude that many teachers were using common sense.

A novel way to imply that teachers are at fault for assigning books at students' reading level, not grade level, can be found in a comment on the Fordham Institute's finding: "Fewer struggling readers are being challenged to catch up to where they should be."[20] Teachers are to blame if they don't assign students reading material above what they can understand. One wonders why Fordham Institute's report doesn't suggest looking critically at the advice given to teachers in their schools or training programs—or asking teachers why they were doing the opposite of what their standards wanted them to do. Instead, it recommends more "supports" for teachers—to implement poor advice:

> First, if we want teachers to assign texts based on students' grade levels—rather than their reading levels—we need to do more to help them bridge the gap between the two. Increasing the complexity of the texts that all students are exposed to is a hallmark of the CCSS-ELA, yet the survey results suggest that there has been serious backsliding in this area since our 2013 report. In our view, the most likely explanation is that teachers lack the supports they need to carry out this portion of their mission.[21]

WHY THE SCHOOL CURRICULUM CHANGED AFTER 1970

Education policy makers didn't create an Alice-in-Wonderland world for K–12 overnight. It took several decades to prepare the ground. The school curriculum changed dramatically over the course of the last half of the twentieth century. The focus was clearly on low achievers after 1965. This meant less emphasis on reading outside of school, more time devoted to writing activities in school, and making all math learning relevant to daily life (justified as "real-world" problem solving). There were lower reading levels for most textbooks, as requested chiefly by teachers themselves in the face of very mixed reading levels in their classes. School administrators and many English teachers eliminated as Eurocentric long books with a high school reading level from the curriculum if they were written by white males and females before 1970. They claimed that an experience-based "reader-response" approach to the interpretation of any genre encouraged a more meaningful interpretation of a literary work and "ownership" by students who were alienated by an analytical approach to what they read.

The psychological reasons for the changes that took place in pedagogy and content in the school curriculum after 1970 are likely the same reasons for the unquestioned acceptance of gap closing as an educational goal in later decades. Many citizens, whether their ancestors were in this country in 1864 or not, felt guilty about the shabby treatment of Southern blacks during and after Reconstruction, Jim Crow laws in the South, and the low achievement of African Americans as a group on all education indexes—continuing until well after the beginning of the twenty-first century.[22] Gap closing was supposed to eliminate the difference in group averages between whites and blacks or Hispanics that showed up everywhere in education statistics on state and federal tests (so long as students were put in categories that didn't show subgroup or generational differences).

Even when low-performing demographic groups improved academically, as in the Bay State between 2005 and 2013, gaps were portrayed as an unacceptable weakness of the state's standards.[23] Increases in academic learning as indicated by higher test scores were conveyed as less important than stubborn gaps (which would likely be there for a long time in the context of rising scores for every demographic group). Congress, education policy makers, and the many organizations that sprang up to "reform" education no longer sought to strengthen education for all students and no longer thought that increasingly higher scores were worth celebrating if gaps weren't narrowing. And, according to the "reformers," gaps always needed to be closed between white students and others, but rarely between high-performing Asian American students and others. Parents were also rarely consulted by education policy makers about parents' priorities: higher scores for all or narrowing gaps.

A lack of financial resources was usually considered the reason for education policy failures, justifying, among other things, the need to reauthorize ESEA throughout the latter half of the twentieth century. Low-income or low-achieving students weren't becoming higher achievers, it was implied, because of inadequate preschool programs and after-school programs; teachers who didn't have good enough preservice or in-service professional training on turning low achievers into higher achievers; inadequate funding, as in the legal judgment in 1985 for the Abbott school districts in New Jersey; and bigoted teachers, schools, and communities.[24] Policy makers defended failed policies without admitting their responsibility by citing one or all of these reasons.

How can policy makers learn from failed policies if the failed policies aren't judged as failed but simply as insufficiently implemented or inadequately funded? How can policy makers learn from successful policies (e.g., the mathematics achievement in Quebec's elementary and secondary schools, Massachusetts's strong academic standards and licensure regulations) if they aren't willing to trade an increase in high school graduation rates for gaps that don't narrow much or an academically stronger pool of teachers?[25]

After 1970, high school graduation rates and grade point averages (GPAs) became even less meaningful than they already were. Grade inflation would enable many teachers to survive if they didn't want to retire soon. That meant, in effect, that many students would be officially eligible for admission to college, even if they really weren't ready for college-level work (or didn't necessarily want to go to college). As suggested previously, a range of "retention" strategies would keep academically unready students in high school or college until they finally completed a degree program. The goal of a stronger K–12 curriculum for all students faded from memory altogether.

SUMMARY

Most teachers and administrators in K–12 have known for decades that an academically stronger curriculum as, for example, in pre–Common Core California and Massachusetts, was *not* the goal of "education reform" in the 1980s, 1990s, and afterward. So, by 2001, one finds few objections to the purpose of the No Child Left Behind Act: "To close the achievement gap with accountability, flexibility, and choice, so that no child is left behind." *Accountability* became the new buzzword. It was the key, its advocates thought, to closing the achievement gap. And it was reasonable to think that all public schools needed to be accountable for the federal education money they received.

However, public schools apparently didn't need to be accountable for local education money or state money that didn't come directly from the federal government. Only the federal government (the Department of Education) knew what needed to be done to close gaps, and it may have decided that it was more important to close gaps than to raise all students academically. Strengthening public education for all children disappeared as a purpose of ESEA, despite its appearance in the original 1965 legislation. The purpose of Title I in 2001 was "improving the academic achievement of the disadvantaged." But this assumed that all other students were already getting an academically strong education.

KEY IDEAS TO REMEMBER

1. The purpose of the Elementary and Secondary Education Act has evolved from strengthening public education and the academic achievement of children in low-income families to closing education gaps among unspecified groups and ensuring an equitable education for all children. It has never been clear what *equitable* means and who determines it. Is it the same amount of money spent per pupil or the same results per pupil, regardless of how much money it takes to get there, as determined by the Department of Education?

2. The Department of Education has issued no guidelines for classroom teachers on exactly how to close gaps, but the language in the Every Student Succeeds Act (ESSA) requires that all state plans include gap-closing standards (called college- and career-ready standards).

3. Many teachers and administrators try to close gaps by teaching less content to all. They also tend to not ask college teaching faculty what college readiness requires, in general or in specific areas.

4. For decades, gap closers have focused on self-esteem as a guiding principle in eliminating policies or programs in a school that cater to differences in intellectual activities between faster and slower students. They believe that such policies as class rankings and valedictorians damage some students' self-esteem.

5. A new addition to the list of activities and programs that *damage* self-esteem is the assignment of reading material at the students' reading level, not grade level (discrimination on intellectual grounds). But this advice does not account for personalized learning.

NOTES

1. Every Student Succeeds Act, 114th Cong., S. 1177 (January 6, 2015), https://www.govinfo.gov/content/pkg/BILLS-114s1177enr/html/BILLS-114s1177enr.htm. According to the Every Student Succeeds Act (section 1001), "the purpose of this title is to provide all children significant opportunity to receive a fair, equitable, and high-quality education, and to close educational achievement gaps."

2. Lawrence M. Berger, Maria Cancian, Eunhee Han, Jennifer Noyes, and Vanessa Rios-Salas, "Children's Academic Achievement and Foster Care," *Pediatrics* 135, no. 1 (January 2015): 109–16, http://pediatrics.aappublications.org/content/pediatrics/135/1/e109.full.pdf; "Students in Foster Care," US Department of Education, last modified June 27, 2016, https://www2.ed.gov/about/inits/ed/foster-care/index.html.

3. Shane Vander Hart, "The Classic Learning Test: An Alternative College Entrance Exam," Truth in American Education, September 28, 2016, https://truthinamericaneducation.com/homeschool-private-school/classic-learning-test-alternative-college-entrance-exam.

4. The Fordham Institute is silent on what teachers should do if a fifth-grader reads at a high school level. See Solomon Friedberg, Diane Barone, Juliana Belding, Andrew Chen, Linda Dixon, Francis (Skip) Fennell, Douglas Fisher, Nancy Frey, Roger Howe, and Tim Shanahan, *The State of State Standards Post-Common Core* (Washington, DC: Thomas Ford-

ham Institute, 2018), 16, https://edexcellence.net/publications/the-state-of-state-standards-post-common-core.

5. Tom Loveless, "The Banality of Deeper Learning," *Brown Center Chalkboard* (blog), May 29, 2013, https://www.brookings.edu/research/the-banality-of-deeper-learning.

6. "Draft Policy Statement on Developing Student Achievement Levels for the National Assessment of Educational Progress," *Federal Register* 83, no. 45618 (September 10, 2018): 45618–19, https://www.federalregister.gov/documents/2018/09/10/2018-19650/draft-policy-statement-on-developing-student-achievement-levels-for-the-national-assessment-of.

7. Sandra Stotsky, "Historians Want to Put Events in Context. Common Core Doesn't. That's a Problem," History News Network, December 24, 2017, https://historynewsnetwork.org/article/167574.

8. "Common Core History Lesson Plans," LTA Toolkit, 2016, https://www.literacyta.com/lesson-plans/history.

9. Tony Fay, "'MCAS 2.0' Proposal Approved by State Board of Education," *WWLP*, November 17, 2015, https://www.wwlp.com/news/massachusetts/state-board-of-education-deciding-on-proposal-for-mcas-2-0/1042677317.

10. "Former MA Official Warns RI about Switch from PARCC to MCAS," *GoLocal LIVE*, May 3, 2017, http://www.golocalprov.com/live/former-ma-official-warns-ri-about-switch-from-parcc-to-mcas; Sandra Stotsky, "How Do You Sell Common Core Standards and Tests to Unwilling Parents? Hide Them," *New Boston Post*, April 19, 2017, https://newbostonpost.com/2017/04/19/how-do-you-sell-common-core-standards-and-tests-to-unwilling-parents-hide-them.

11. Sandra Stotsky, "Is Common Core Racist? Check Out the Results," *New Boston Post*, May 9, 2018, https://newbostonpost.com/2018/05/09/is-common-core-racist-check-out-the-results.

12. Camille L. Ryan and Kurt Bauman, *Education Attainment in the United States: 2015, Population Characteristics, Current Population Reports* (Washington, DC: US Department of Commerce Economics and Statistics Administration, March 2016), https://www.census.gov/content/dam/Census/library/publications/2016/demo/p20-578.pdf.

13. "Are Dual-Credit Courses Helping Poor, Minority Students in Texas?" editorial, *Dallas News*, August 10, 2018, https://www.dallasnews.com/opinion/editorials/2018/08/10/dual-credit-courses-helping-poor-minority-students-texas.

14. Alexandra W. Logue, "The Extensive Evidence of Co-Requisite Remediation's Effectiveness," *Inside Higher Ed* (July 17, 2018), https://www.insidehighered.com/views/2018/07/17/data-already-tell-us-how-effective-co-requisite-education-opinion.

15. Maggie Lit, "The Average College Freshman Reads at 7th Grade Level," Campus Reform, January 6, 2015, https://www.campusreform.org/?ID=6174.

16. Laurisa White Reyes, "Motivating the Low-Achieving Teen," Education.com, May 27, 2014, https://www.education.com/magazine/article/Motivating_the_Low-Achieving.

17. Jamie Amemiya and Ming-Te Wang, "Why Effort Praise Can Backfire in Adolescence," *Child Development Perspectives* 12, no. 3 (September 2018): 199–203, https://onlinelibrary.wiley.com/doi/full/10.1111/cdep.12284.

18. Albert Mohler, "The Self-Esteem Movement Backfires—When Praise Is Dangerous," Albert Mohler, February 15, 2007, https://albertmohler.com/2007/02/16/the-self-esteem-movement-backfires-when-praise-is-dangerous.

19. David Griffith and Ann Duffett, *Reading and Writing Instruction in America's Schools* (Washington, DC: Thomas B. Fordham Institute, 2018), https://edexcellence.net/publications/reading-and-writing-instruction-in-americas-schools.

20. Carolyn Phenicie, "New Study of Common Core Reading Standards Finds Teachers Aren't Giving Students Appropriately Challenging Texts," The 74, July 19, 2018, https://www.the74million.org/article/new-study-of-common-core-reading-standards-finds-teachers-arent-giving-students-appropriately-challenging-texts.

21. Griffith and Duffett, *Reading and Writing Instruction*.

22. Ben Chapman, "Critics Blast City for Hiding Study That Debunks de Blasio's Plan to Desegregate Elite High Schools," *New York Daily News*, August 6, 2018, http://www.

nydailynews.com/new-york/education/ny-metro-critics-blast-city-for-hiding-desegregation-study-20180806-story.html.

23. "Achievement Gap," Citizens for Public Schools, 2019, https://www.citizensforpublicschools.org/achievement-gap.

24. Wikipedia Contributors, "Abbott District," Wikipedia, last updated October 3, 2018, https://en.wikipedia.org/w/index.php?title=Abbott_district&oldid=862336996.

25. Paul W. Bennett, "What Can Be Learned from Quebec's Math Prowess?" Policy Options, October 23, 2018, http://policyoptions.irpp.org/magazines/october-2018/what-can-be-learned-from-quebecs-math-prowess.

Chapter Ten

How to Begin Altering the Roots of Low Achievement

Educators have not explored two factors influencing academic achievement in the past half-century. Most readers would probably agree that a student's own effort deserves much more attention than it has gotten for its influence on a student's academic achievement. But doesn't a student's civic identity, especially in the age of identity politics, play a similar role? That is what this final chapter also claims, and it concludes with suggestions to state legislatures and Congress on what they might do to begin altering the roots of low achievement in this country. Parents have had their hands tied by administrators in their local schools, trained to ignore parents' wishes and complaints and pass the buck to their state education agency.

Beyond the Classroom: Why School Reform Has Failed and What Parents Need to Do, by Laurence Steinberg, a psychology professor, and several colleagues, should remind all of us in the second decade of the twenty-first century how long it has been since anyone explained clearly to the public why widespread low achievement in high school has not been solved by "school reform," however defined. In fact, no recognized twenty-first-century "reformers" have bothered to explain to the public or their funding sources why their attempts at school reform have had so little success. A common excuse is that their reforms (like "personalized learning") for increasing the achievement of all students (especially low achievers) were not implemented adequately. But were the obstacles not enough money for the necessary technology and bigoted communities?

The authors of *Beyond the Classroom* do not look at low-income students or those defined as low achievers by federal or state policy makers. They do not compare politically defined ethnic and racial groups with a white norm (and then demean the norm). They look at all American students and see low achievement in most high school students—something we no longer hear from education policy makers, who believe that higher achievers in K–12 are actually high achievers. Higher achievers in recent decades have not been high achievers. Most were simply higher than those who were, by definition, academically lower. Decline in high achievement started in the 1960s.

As understood by the authors of the Massachusetts Education Reform Act of 1993, as well as by the authors of the federal Elementary and Secondary Education Act in 1965 and major commentators on education after World War II, all American students needed to improve academically, especially lower achievers and the children of low-income families (the two groups were interchangeable for education policy makers). Educators who understood curriculum knew that it and many teachers in public schools needed to be strengthened.

The National Defense Education Act (NDEA) was Congress's response to the Soviet launching of *Sputnik* in 1957. The K–12 curriculum needed to become more demanding for all students, not just for low achievers or low-income students. The institutes funded by the NDEA, which was passed by Congress in 1958, were organized by teachers and subject-area academic experts to reform and update the entire K–12 curriculum in mathematics, science, and foreign languages.

Unfortunately, NDEA-related activities didn't last long—a little over a decade, ending approximately around 1970. The curricular goals of the NDEA participants were mostly ignored as federal and state legislators and major philanthropists turned their attention and funding away from the K–12 curriculum and the reform of content-related pedagogy and toward chiefly those students struggling in school, no matter the curriculum. The struggling students needed attention, everyone knew. So did the K–12 curriculum. But no one felt guilty about giving struggling students a weak K–12 curriculum. Indeed, many reformers thought a weaker school curriculum was the way to help struggling students.

Efforts to address the reading problems of struggling students, especially minority children, had already begun to suck up all the oxygen in the public schools before 1965, and whatever degree of rigor the school curriculum had after World War II had already begun to dissipate as part of a long, slow academic decline. In English, the decline in coherence began when the year-long high school English class was divided into two semesters (most high school subjects had long been taught in year-long courses), and English teachers often were able to choose what they wanted to teach in a semester elective. Coherence vanished wherever students could choose what they wanted to read and write about.

Not only did educators in schools of education *not* know how to address the problems embedded in massive low achievement, but they also didn't care to know that many of the reading remedies they were imposing on the schools in the decades after World War II (such as "multicultural" education) were worsening the education of low-achieving minority students. Many low achievers, unlike low achievers in most nineteenth-century schools, were not perceived as sharing a civic identity with other members of their culture. Instead, they were perceived as members of a different culture, with language differences. Their history curriculum was becoming as corrupted as their English curriculum had been.

Steinberg's book reports a study by collaborative teams from three universities that surveyed thousands of high school students, their parents, friends, teachers, and school administrators across the country. Steinberg and his team conclude, as do the authors of the 1966 Coleman and 1965 Moynihan reports, that the greatest influence on students' classroom performance is their parents. It found their friends almost as influential. The book's central conclusions are noted in the many reviews of the book, most of which were published in major publications for education professionals. A 2003 review comments, "Laurence Steinberg and colleagues surveyed more than 20,000 students and found that Asian students, who outscored all others in measures of school engagement, were also more likely to have friends (whether Asian or not) who emphasized success in school. For black and Hispanic students, Steinberg's findings were the opposite."[1] Notice that students have already been classified as members of a range of cultures and ethnic or racial groups.

Steinberg also notes that the qualities leading to school engagement by Asian students could be fostered by parents of other students and lead to the same results: "A more reasonable reading of the evidence is that Asian students perform better in school because they work harder, try harder, and are more interested in achievement—the very same factors that contribute to school success among *all* ethnic groups."[2] Surprisingly, *student effort* is not addressed in the Coleman and Moynihan reports or the various reauthorizations of the Elementary and Secondary Education Act (including No Child Left Behind in 2001 and Every Student Succeeds Act in 2015). Perhaps educated researchers assumed that all students were still being taught that they were equal members of our civic culture, regardless of academic achievement, and shared the same level of school engagement, but student effort wasn't explored earlier.

By the beginning of the twenty-first century, it was clear to education writers (whether they conveyed the message consistently or not) that schools were not only *not* the cause of low achievement but that schools were *not* the solution, either. One website succinctly explains why K–12 teachers could *not* be the cause of the academic achievement gap in US public schools:

> Research shows that the achievement gap, which often first manifests itself through standardized tests in elementary school, actually begins well before students reach kindergarten as a "school readiness" gap. One study claims that

about half the test score gap between black and white high school students is already evident when children start school. A variety of different tests at kindergarten entry have provided evidence of such a gap, including the U.S. Department of Education's Early Childhood Longitudinal Survey of Kindergarten children (ECLS-K). While results differ depending on the instrument, estimates of the black–white gap range from slightly less than half a standard deviation to slightly more than 1 standard deviation.

This early disparity in performance is critical, as research shows that once students are behind, they do not catch up. Children who score poorly on tests of cognitive skills before starting kindergarten are highly likely to be low performers throughout their school careers. The evidence of the early appearance of the gap has led to efforts focused on early childhood interventions.[3]

INEFFECTIVE PRESCHOOL PROGRAMS

Most early childhood interventions have been academically ineffective in the long run. Despite the federal and state money appropriated for Head Start and other public preschool programs, this country has been unable to scale up the few effective preschool programs that emerged from the hundreds subsidized by federal and state funds.

We find vague hints that only a few were effective in the report "The Current State of Scientific Knowledge on Pre-Kindergarten Effects" by an interdisciplinary group of education researchers. After a careful look at the evidence on the impact of state-funded pre-kindergarten programs, the reviewers summarize,

> Convincing evidence shows that children attending a diverse array of state and school district pre-k programs are more ready for school at the end of their pre-k year than children who do not attend pre-k. Improvements in academic areas such as literacy and numeracy are most common; the smaller number of studies of social-emotional and self-regulatory development generally show more modest improvements in those areas.
>
> Convincing evidence on the longer-term impacts of scaled-up pre-k programs on academic outcomes and school progress is sparse, precluding broad conclusions. The evidence that does exist often shows that pre-k-induced improvements in learning are detectable during elementary school, but studies also reveal null or negative longer-term impacts for some programs.[4]

In sum, the reviewers not only do *not* tease out factors that contribute to effectiveness, but they also imply that there may be problems lurking in some of these preschool programs. However, they do not explain what any of these problems are. In fact, they word their conclusions very carefully to avoid suggesting an end to large-scale funding of preschool programs but can't find adequate evidence to support their continued existence. Instead, they simply beg off by saying there is not much "convincing evidence" to justify continuation of support. In other words, caveat emptor!

In response to this study, a pediatrician concludes, "Our current knowledge is insufficient to justify a large expansion of pre-K as the best path forward. . . . There still really is no or very little evidence of effectiveness beyond the actual pre-school year."[5] Remarkably, federal and state policy makers today, perhaps in desperation, call for large-scale expansion of pre-school programs without asking researchers to spell out possible causes of the "negative impacts" or warnings to state and local educators about what to look for. Nevertheless, the basic message of this 2017 study is, Small-scale piloting of different models is still the best way to go. And it's the best way to limit promises.

Should educators or others who implement preschool programs on a large scale without warning the public at large be subject to malpractice lawsuits if long-term academic gains don't materialize and if undesirable school habits appear? If pharmaceutical companies must indicate in their advertisements all the unintended negative effects possible for a drug, then shouldn't those who fund preschool programs, knowing that some will have defects, also be required to indicate what parents and educators should look out for? State legislators and educators need to discuss this issue before passing bills and bonds for preschool programs.

INEFFECTIVE AFTER-SCHOOL PROGRAMS

Are after-schools programs part of the overall solution to low achievement? Only, it seems, if researchers can identify the factors that affect children positively, no matter the kind of after-school they attend. According to recent reports, more than eight million K–12 children participate in after-school programs, so these can be an important part of an education system.

But the best that reviewers can say is that some studies have found small but significant effects of after-school program participation on reading and mathematics achievement and on personal and social skills.[6] In fact, several large-scale evaluations of federally funded after-school programs, called 21st Century Community Learning Centers, found no effects on student academic achievement among elementary and middle school students.

In sum, results from research on the effects of after-school programs on both social and academic outcomes are so mixed and the overall effects, when positive, are so small that researchers are trying to identify factors that *may* explain how participation in after-school programs affects student outcomes positively, even if they cannot be sure and even if all programs do not show positive results. Common sense alone suggests that, until it is clearer why some programs have positive effects on academic and social outcomes, schools should hesitate before investing in social and emotional learning (SEL) on a large scale. What is the likelihood that common sense will prevail?

There is a hint that the teachers in after-school programs may make a difference. One study found, not surprisingly, that after-school staff need specific content knowledge and instructional strategies to facilitate learning. (It is unclear *if* the studies looked at the staff's academic qualifications.) While the reviewers try to assure readers that all staff do not need to be certified teachers, the finding does mean that, "if the goal is to improve reading comprehension, then staff members need to know specific strategies that will help students comprehend what they read."[7]

The reviewers also agree that it is not enough to have after-school staff simply supervise homework completion in small classes. So, what kind of people should schools hire to staff after-school programs? Teachers? Volunteers? Aides? In the final analysis, this important point was not clarified. All in all, the significant features of after-school programs are a big unknown.

In the final chapter of *Beyond the Classroom*, Steinberg observes,

> Today's students know less, and can do less, than their counterparts could twenty-five years ago. Our high school graduates are among the least intellectually competent in the industrialized world. Contrary to widespread claims that the low achievement of American students is not real—that it is merely a "statistical artifact"—systematic scientific evidence indicates quite compellingly that the problem of poor student achievement is genuine, substantial, and pervasive across ethnic, socio-economic and age groups.[8]

Few would disagree, then and today, that student achievement in American schools is lower than it should or could be. So why, one must ask, was the 2015 authorization of the Elementary and Secondary Education Act (ESSA) concerned with gap closing, not strengthening public education for all, regardless if gaps are closed? And why haven't state plans required by ESSA promoted school engagement in the form of disciplined activity by students *inside of* school—instead of civic engagement or political activity by students *outside of* school? And why weren't state departments of education asked to address student effort in their state plans?[9]

STUDENT ENGAGEMENT WITH SCHOOL

School engagement is rarely used today to describe the bundle of characteristics wanted in all students, yet it may be a much more appropriate goal for early childhood educators than "academic achievement," even when it includes activities in reading and arithmetic aimed at academic achievement. Another virtue of school engagement is that it can also be demonstrated by low-performing students who remain low achievers but come to school regularly and follow a teacher's directions. As Wikipedia describes,

> Student engagement is frequently used to "depict students' willingness to participate in routine school activities, such as attending class, submitting required work, and following teachers' directions in class." It occurs when "students make a psychological investment in learning. They try hard to learn what school offers. They take pride not simply in earning the formal indicators of success (grades), but in understanding the material and incorporating or internalizing it in their lives.". . . The term is often used to refer as much to student involvement in extra-curricular activities in the life of a school/college/university which are thought to have educational benefits as it is to student focus on their curricular studies. [10]

It seems safe to say that school engagement is the kind of socialization the public expects a preschool, kindergarten, or primary-grade teacher to shape. It is also the kind of socialization expected in a preschool or higher grades that may be difficult for teachers to achieve today because an increasing number of students in K–12 come from families that do not see themselves sharing an identity with their neighbors and most others in our civic culture or whose children may behave differently from those in intact families. [11]

Students are unlikely to become college- and career-ready in higher grades until they are first socialized for the routines of a normal school day in earlier grades. Yet, boosting school engagement alone does not lead to higher academic performance. [12]

What does lead to higher academic performance? We have one major example to learn from at a statewide level—the Bay State. All demographic groups for K–12 students in Massachusetts made academic gains from 2003 to 2013—gains that for the most part endured. Surprisingly, few education policy makers or researchers have tried to identify the distinctive features of the Bay State's highly praised standards in those years, interview the staff responsible for their effectiveness, or search for other large-scale influences on student learning that might also account for the high scores on such tests as NAEP and TIMSS that could not be manipulated by Bay State policy makers.

NOT-SO-SECRET INGREDIENTS IN THE BAY STATE'S PRE–COMMON CORE STANDARDS

Chapter 7 provides a detailed description of and evaluative comments from outsiders on the features of the Bay State's pre–Common Core English language arts standards. The following is a summary by Sheila Byrd Carmichael, Kathleen Porter-Magee, and other reviewers in the *State of State Standards—and the Common Core—in 2010*, released by the Thomas B. Fordham Institute on July 21, 2010. That was the day the Bay State's board of education voted to get rid of the state's pre–Common Core standards and replace them with a controversial and untested set of standards—Common Core:

> Massachusetts's existing standards are clearer, more thorough, and easier to read than the Common Core standards. Essential content is grouped more logically, so that standards addressing inextricably linked characteristics, such as themes in literary texts, can be found together rather than spread across strands. In addition, Massachusetts frequently uses standard-specific examples to clarify expectations. Unlike the Common Core, Massachusetts's standards treat both literary and non-literary texts in systematic detail throughout the document, addressing the specific genres, sub-genres, and characteristics of both text types. While both sets of standards address American literature and append lists of exemplar texts, Massachusetts's reading list is far more comprehensive. Standards addressing vocabulary development and grammar are also more detailed and rigorous in the Massachusetts document. [13]

Aside from the laudatory comments for the Bay State's pre–Common Core ELA standards by Fordham Institute's reviewers, these standards are worth adopting by other states and readopting by the Bay State. Before they were eliminated in 2010 by its state board of education, the Bay State's pre–Common Core standards (2001 and 2004 for ELA, 2000 for mathematics) helped to accomplish in the state the following:

> On the 2005, 2007, 2009, 2011, and 2013 tests given by NAEP, Massachusetts students had the highest average scores in grades 4 and 8 in both mathematics and reading. The scores of the state's low-income students, compared with those in other states on NAEP's 2007 tests (the only year for which there is a demographic breakdown across states), were tied for first place in grades 4 and 8 mathematics and in grade 4 reading. In grade 8 reading, they were tied for second place. For results on international tests in mathematics and science (TIMSS) given in 2007 and 2013, Massachusetts 4th graders ranked second worldwide in science achievement and tied for third in mathematics; the state's 8th graders tied for first in science and ranked sixth in mathematics. The Bay State percent of public high school students passing Advanced Placement courses with a 3 or more is a larger percentage than in most other states in the nation and well above the national average of 15.2 percent. [14]

One might think at first that the praise given by Fordham Institute reviewers for the Bay State's pre–Common Core vocabulary and grammar standards ("more detailed and rigorous") would have stimulated broader use (or at least their retention in the Bay State). Nevertheless, the Massachusetts Department of Elementary and Secondary Education was unsuccessful in getting the standards writers to insert them into Common Core's English language arts and reading document while it was being developed in 2009 and 2010. Staff at the department tried more than once. It didn't matter whether the document acknowledged the Massachusetts Department of Education or no one at all. Common Core's writers wanted nothing to do with vocabulary and grammar standards from Massachusetts in 2009, anonymous or not.

Nor did Common Core's writers want to draw on other features of the 2001 document, mentioned in a talk by their chief architect, Sandra Stotsky, to the Wakefield (New Hampshire) School Board in 2014 after it had voted to adopt the Bay State's pre–Common Core standards.[15] Indeed, there was nothing to indicate that the Bay State's English teachers themselves wanted standards different from the pre–Common Core standards they had been teaching since 2001.

The Bay State's board of education did not invite groups of high school English teachers to explain what they would now have to teach (once Common Core's standards were adopted) and how the entire reading and literature curriculum would have to be changed. Diane Ravitch made it clear in *Education Week* in 2006 that "50 standards for 50 states" was a formula for incoherence and obfuscation.[16] It seemed that states could not have their own standards, *especially* if they were visibly stronger or potentially more effective than Common Core's.

Why, then, one might wonder, did Common Core's own ELA standards receive a grade of B+ from the Fordham Institute?[17] Given the deficiencies in Common Core's ELA standards pointed out by Fordham Institute's own reviewers in its 2010 monograph, it is a remarkable exercise of the imagination to suggest that Common Core's ELA standards *earned* a B+, a verb that Fordham Institute often repeated in the *Bottom Line* of its 2010 reviews for the fifty states. A well-trained English teacher probably would have given its ELA standards a D+.

But reporters and state departments of education did not pay attention to what the academic critics on Common Core's own Validation Committee (James Milgram, Sandra Stotsky, and Arthur Applebee, in particular) were saying publicly about Common Core's standards. Did they have to depend on the "grades" given by the only organization in the country grading state standards because they couldn't evaluate them on their own?

It's too bad they didn't quote Jason Zimba, Common Core's lead mathematics writer, who was reported in the official minutes of a public meeting of the Massachusetts Board of Elementary and Secondary Education in March 2010 as saying, "The concept of college readiness is minimal and focuses on non-selective colleges."[18] Zimba exemplifies his statement in many ways, such as "the minimally college-ready student is a student who passed Algebra II."

Until reporters, education researchers, and state departments of education can appropriately evaluate standards documents and the standards themselves, they would serve policy makers better by not repeating or stressing, how "rigorous" these standards are, especially when Common Core's standards appear to be contributing to a national decline in academic achievement.[19]

FINALE: ALTERING THE ROOTS
OF LOW ACHIEVEMENT

How can the roots of low achievement be altered in 2019? Most state legislatures can legally require:

1. Establishment of locally developed high school standards for all subjects taught in their high schools, as well as locally developed end-of-course tests for these standards, vetted and corrected only by high school and college teaching faculty in their own state.
2. Hiring of local teachers who have passed state-developed tests of demanding subject matter, to accord with the research finding by the Task Force on Teacher Education (members of the National Mathematics Advisory Panel) that the only characteristics of an effective teacher found in high-quality research are verbal skills and mastery of the subject(s) taught.[20]

As a complement, Congress can legally:

1. Declare the four-year state education plans approved by the Department of Education as unconstitutional (which they are) on the grounds that they are associated with widening gaps in academic achievement.[21]
2. Require teacher-preparation programs wanting federal loans and grants to teach only pedagogical strategies that have demonstrably improved student achievement and to encourage new teachers and schools to adopt only such reading programs as Direct Instruction, which can show long-term growth.[22]
3. End congressional funding of all research related to ESEA and gap-closing standards and fund research related to *Race, Class, and Family Intervention: Engaging Parents and Families for Academic Success* by William Sampson.[23]
4. Forbid data collection that sorts American students or their families by race, ethnicity, home language, and religious creed.
5. Fund K–12 civic-education programs (e.g., Center for Civic Education) that restore students' understanding of who they are as individuals in this country's civic culture.

So where, one might ask, does a student's civic identity fit into this picture and contribute today to low achievement? In the much-neglected history curriculum that has been hijacked and smothered by contemporary standards for the English language arts. There have always been many reasons for a history curriculum in the public schools. The transformation of a K–12 history curriculum into a litany of grievances against the founding itself has taken its toll on the most vulnerable groups of youngsters in our society. An increasing number of students are growing up without a sense of membership in their country's civic culture. Young Americans are less likely than older Americans to believe that they have a shared identity and membership in a culture based on political equality.

A civic education, as defined by education historian R. Freeman Butts, meant explicit and continuing study of the basic concepts and values underlying this country's democratic political community and constitutional order.[24] What mattered at the end of a K–12 public education was not whether a student was college-ready or career-ready but whether individual students were ready to participate in their local, state, and national culture as informed citizens and to view others who participated with them as fellow citizens with a shared identity as intended by the Fourteenth Amendment to the Constitution.

Only an education in what informed participation in a civic culture requires, not an academic education driven by the notion of gap closing, can begin to undo the damage created by the label "low achiever" and the goal of closing gaps. A coherent K–12 history curriculum no longer exists in our public schools. Students no longer learn about the political principles underlying a federal form of government and what they share as members of a rich culture, judging from the content of the social studies standards now being adopted for K–12 schools and teacher preparation.[25] Instead, they are given a fragmented sweep of world history, divided by continents, centuries, and cultures studded with proper nouns most students cannot pronounce.

The pre–Common Core US history curriculum, which in effect was a major part of the curriculum for civic education in public schools, was the only place where low achievers learned that informed participation in our culture was the goal of public education and that all citizens were politically equal, regardless of academic achievement. That ideal has been abandoned, if not lost. It badly needs to be restored as the explicit goal of public education and newly revised Common Core standards if we are to begin altering the roots of low achievement and fostering civic unity.

NOTES

1. Anne Rogers Poliakoff, "Closing the Gap: An Overview," *ASCD Info Brief* 44 (January): 1–10, http://www.ascd.org/publications/newsletters/policy-priorities/jan06/num44/toc.aspx.
2. Laurence Steinberg, *Beyond the Classroom: Why School Reform Has Failed and What Parents Need to Do* (New York: Simon & Schuster, 1997), 86–87.

3. "Origins and Causes of the Achievement Gap," K12 Academics, 2019, https://www.k12academics.com/achievement-gap-united-states/origins-causes-achievement-gap.

4. Deborah A. Phillips, Mark W. Lipsey, Kenneth A. Dodge, Ron Haskins, Daphna Bassok, Margaret R. Burchinal, Greg J. Duncan, Mark Dynarski, Katherine A. Magnuson, and Christina Weiland, *Puzzling It Out: The Current State of Scientific Knowledge on Pre-Kindergarten Effects: A Consensus Statement* (Washington, DC: Brookings Institution, 2017), https://www.brookings.edu/wp-content/uploads/2017/04/duke_prekstudy_final_4-4-17_hires.pdf.

5. Karen R. Effrem. "Government Preschools Don't Work. So Why Are We Still Funding Them?" *National Pulse*, April 21, 2017, https://thenationalpulse.com/commentary/government-preschools-dont-work-taxpayers-funding.

6. Kathryn E. Grogan, Christopher C. Henrich, and Mariya V. Malikina, "Student Engagement in After-School Programs, Academic Skills, and Social Competence Among Elementary School Students," *Child Development Research*, no. 498506 (2014), https://www.hindawi.com/journals/cdr/2014/498506/.

7. Nancy Protheroe, "Successful After-school Programs," *Principal* (May/June 2006): 35, https://www.naesp.org/sites/default/files/resources/2/Principal/2006/M-Jp34.pdf.

8. Steinberg, *Beyond the Classroom*.

9. Jessica Fries-Gaither, "Effort, Praise, and Achievement: What Research Says to the Elementary Teacher," Beyond Penguins and Polar Bears, February 2010, https://beyondpenguins.ehe.osu.edu/issue/polar-explorers/effort-praise-and-achievement-what-research-says-to-the-elementary-teacher.

10. "School Engagement," Wikipedia, updated March 16, 2019, https://en.wikipedia.org/wiki/Student_engagement.

11. Patrick F. Fagan (ed.), "Effects of Marriage on Children's Education," Marripedia, http://marripedia.org/effects.of.marriage.on.children.s.education. According to studies published by 2012 on factors related to the effects of marriage on children's education,

> Children of married parents are more engaged in school than children from all other family structures. Children from intact families have fewer behavioral problems in school. First-grade children born to married mothers are less likely to exhibit disruptive behavior, such as disobeying a teacher or behaving aggressively towards peers, than children born to cohabiting or single mothers. Adolescents from intact married families are less frequently suspended, expelled, or delinquent, and less frequently experience school problems than children from other family structures.

12. Tom Loveless, "Part III: Student Engagement," in *The 2015 Brown Center Report on American Education: How Well Are American Students Learning?* (Washington, DC: Brookings Institution, 2015), 26–36, https://www.brookings.edu/research/student-engagement.

13. Thomas B. Fordham Institute, "Massachusetts," in *The State of State Standards—and the Common Core—in 2010* (Washington, DC: Thomas B. Fordham Institute, 2010), 162–71, http://edexcellencemedia.net/publications/2010/201007_state_education_standards_common_standards/Massachusetts.pdf.

14. Wikipedia Contributors, "Sandra Stotsky," Wikipedia, updated January 17, 2016, https://en.wikipedia.org/wiki/Sandra_Stotsky.

15. Sandra Stotsky, "What Wakefield, NH's School Board Is Doing to Ensure a First-Rate Education for All Its Students," *Pioneer Institute* (blog), July 17, 2014, https://pioneerinstitute.org/blog/what-wakefield-nhs-school-board-is-doing-to-ensure-a-first-rate-education-for-all-its-students.

16. "Quality Counts at 10: A Decade of Standards-Based Education," *Education Week* 25, no. 17 (2006), https://www.edweek.org/ew/toc/2006/01/05/index.html.

17. Thomas B. Fordham Institute, *The State of State Standards—and the Common Core—in 2010* (Washington, DC: Thomas B. Fordham Institute, 2010), https://fordhaminstitute.org/national/research/state-state-standards-and-common-core-2010.

18. Editorial Staff, "Video: Lead Mathematics Standards-Writer Jason Zimba," Pioneer Institute, October 10, 2013, https://pioneerinstitute.org/news/video-common-core-lead-writer-

jason-zimba; NoTo CommonCore, "Jason Zimba Interacts with Dr. Sandra Stotsky," YouTube, October 2, 2013, https://www.youtube.com/watch?v=eJZY4mh2rt8.

19. ACT, *Condition of College and Career Readiness, National 2018* (Iowa City: ACT, 2018), http://www.act.org/content/act/en/research/condition-of-college-and-career-readiness-2018.html; Catherine Gewertz, "Math Scores Slide to a 20-Year Low on ACT," *Education Week* (October 17, 2018), https://www.edweek.org/ew/articles/2018/10/17/math-scores-slide-to-a-20-year-low.html#comments.

20. Deborah Loewenberg Ball, James Simons, Hung-Hsi Wu, Raymond Simon, Grover J. "Russ" Whitehurst, and Jim Yun, "Chapter 5: Report of the Task Group on Teachers and Teacher Education," in *Foundations for Success: The Final Report of the National Mathematics Advisory Panel* (Washington, DC: US Department of Education, 2008), 5–7, https://www2.ed.gov/about/bdscomm/list/mathpanel/report/teachers.pdf; National Mathematics Advisory Panel, *Foundations for Success: The Final Report of the National Mathematics Advisory Panel* (Washington, DC: US Department of Education, 2008), https://www2.ed.gov/about/bdscomm/list/mathpanel/report/final-report.pdf.

21. Jane Robbins, "New Evidence Reveals Full Extent of Common Core's Historic Failure," Townhall, November 20, 2018, https://townhall.com/columnists/janerobbins/2018/11/20/new-evidence-reveals-full-extent-of-common-cores-historic-failure-n2536233.

22. "Curriculum Overview," Thales Academy, 2018, https://www.thalesacademy.org/academics/curriculum-overview; Lauren Ingeno, "Teacher Ed Takedown," *Inside Higher Ed*, June 18, 2013, https://www.insidehighered.com/news/2013/06/18/nctq-study-gives-teacher-prep-programs-failing-grades. For a critique of US schools of education, see Arthur Levine, "Educating School Teachers," Education Schools Project, 2006, https://eric.ed.gov/?id=ED504135.

23. William A. Sampson, *Race, Class, and Family Intervention: Engaging Parents and Families for Academic Success* (Lanham, MD: Rowman & Littlefield Education, 2007).

24. "TC Emeritus Professor R. Freeman Butts, Education Historian and Philosopher, Dies at 99," press release, Teachers College, March 23, 2010, https://www.tc.columbia.edu/articles/2010/march/tc-emeritus-professor-r-freeman-butts-education-historian-/. For further details, see Henry Kiernan, *Teaching Civic Identity and Civic Writing in the Information Age* (Washington, DC: ERIC Clearinghouse, 1990), https://files.eric.ed.gov/fulltext/ED348339.pdf; Sandra Stotsky, *The Connections between Language Education and Civic Education* (Bloomington, IN: ERIC Clearinghouse for Social Studies/Social Science Education, 1992), https://www.ericdigests.org/1992-2/civic.htm; Sandra Stotsky, "How Should American Students Understand Their Civic Culture," Education News, March 30, 2016, http://www.educationviews.org/american-students-understand-civic-culture; and the ERIC Clearinghouse collection of writings by Sandra Stotsky, https://eric.ed.gov/?q=%22%22&ff1=subCivics&ff2=autStotsky%2c+Sandra.

25. National Council for the Social Studies Task Force on Teacher Education Standards, *National Standards for the Preparation of Social Studies Teachers* (Silver Spring, MD: National Council for the Social Studies, 2018), https://www.socialstudies.org/sites/default/files/media/2017/Nov/ncss_teacher_standards_2017-rev9-6-17.pdf.

About the Author

Sandra Stotsky is professor of education emerita at the University of Arkansas, where she held the Twenty-First-Century Chair in Teacher Quality. She served as senior associate commissioner at the Massachusetts Department of Elementary and Secondary Education from 1999 to 2003, where she was in charge of developing and revising the state's K–12 standards, teacher licensure tests, and teacher and administrator licensure regulations.

Stotsky served on the Common Core Validation Committee from 2009 to 2010 and did not sign off on Common Core's standards because they were not rigorous, internationally benchmarked, or research based. From 1991 to 1997, she was editor of the premier research journal *Research in the Teaching of English*, published by the National Council of Teachers of English. She has taught at the elementary, secondary, undergraduate, and graduate levels; published extensively in professional journals; and written and contributed to several books.

Stotsky was appointed to the Massachusetts Board of Elementary and Secondary Education in 2006 and served until 2010. She served as a town meeting member in Brookline from 1984 to 1994 and as a trustee of the public library from 1984 to 1999. She was president of the Brookline League of Women Voters from 1971 to 1973. Stotsky received her undergraduate degree in French literature from the University of Michigan and her graduate degree in reading research and reading education from the Harvard Graduate School of Education in 1976.

Made in the USA
San Bernardino, CA
11 June 2020